Advance Praise

The education sector has found its answer to scalability and impact in the form of education technology or edtech. India has developed a rich entrepreneurial culture and many unicorns, especially in the edtech space, are waiting to happen. Indian players, such as, UpGrad, are trying to tap into various segments of it. Right from K12 to learning and development about emotions management, there is enough potential for entrepreneurs to embrace and win over the "hurricanes" of challenges. As a believer and supporter of edtech, I do believe that Rishi's book is a very thoughtful compilation of the journey of early stage entrepreneurs. It lays out the experiences and frameworks that can be adopted for reducing their time to market and revenue. I wish them all luck.

Ronnie Screwvala,
Entrepreneur, Philanthropist and Author

Rishi has penned an authoritative guide on entrepreneurship, straddling both its theory and practice. Information I wish I had while we were building MakeMyTrip. A highly recommended read for students, educators and young VCs & entrepreneurs.

Sachin Bhatia,
Co-founder and ex-CMO, MakeMyTrip,
Co-founder and CEO, TrulyMadly

Rishi's book is very well done. The minute I started with writing a contribution in the chapters, I knew exactly what they wanted to convey. I have studied the entrepreneurship ecosystem for many years and Rishi's book captures the real value drivers for startups to be able to adopt and scale up. The book is a delightful guide full of relevant information for those who want to create great companies and make true meaning.

Sachin Tagra,
Head, Capital18, Network18 Group

I believe that education will change more in the next 20 years than it has in the last 2,000. There is an army of entrepreneurs hurling ideas and innovations at the fortress of traditional systems and the walls are cracking. Globally, we have gone from only 80 companies per year who received venture capital funding in 2008 to now thousands of new venture-back edtech companies every year. Some surveys count a total of more than 10,000 edtech companies propelling change. Rishi Kapal has penned a compelling book about the trials and tribulations of some of these entrepreneurs on their journey for innovation and impact. The lessons learned are invaluable.

Don Burton,
Managing Partner, LearnStart/Learn Capital

The best entrepreneurs know that every great business is built around revenue generation and a conducive ecosystem. Great companies that can change the world by edtech need hand holding at all levels. I have personally supported Rishi's endeavors at EDUGILD and his writing is honest, truthful, and with real-life experiences. My job involves keeping a hawk's eye on the employment and corporate development sector. I find a lot of synergy and relevance with the work that Rishi has penned in his book. Good luck to him.

A. G. Rao,
Group Managing Director, Manpower Group

Access to education has been a utopian dream for millions of aspiring middle- and lower-class people in India. With the advent of technology, edtech has helped democratize the opportunity to learn and has ensured that education for all and from anywhere can in fact be the new reality. Rishi's keen observations will help advance this burgeoning ecosystem by encouraging first-time entrepreneurs to ask the right questions, solve for big problems, and learn from others' mistakes. There can be no better guide than first-hand experience.

Sachin Kapoor,
Head of India and South East Asia
Business Development, LinkedIn

Kites in a Hurricane is a compelling story of the journey of becoming an entrepreneur. Kapal's book is not a how-to guide, but an engaging story that includes interesting characters (the entrepreneurs), an intriguing setting (India), conflict (the pivots needed to succeed), a plot (the steps to rise to the top and stand out) and a theme (the passion for the problem and the solution). The book goes from "a subconscious wow to a tornado moment". A story every hopeful entrepreneur needs to read.

Dr Barbara "Bobbi" Kurshan,
Senior Fellow and Innovation Advisor, Graduate School of
Education, University of Pennsylvania

KITES IN A HURRICANE

KITES IN A HURRICANE

Startups
from Cradle to Fame

RISHI KAPAL

Los Angeles | London | New Delhi
Singapore | Washington DC | Melbourne

First published in 2018 by

SAGE Publications India Pvt Ltd
B1/I-1 Mohan Cooperative Industrial Area
Mathura Road, New Delhi 110 044, India
www.sagepub.in

SAGE Publications Inc
2455 Teller Road
Thousand Oaks, California 91320, USA

SAGE Publications Ltd
1 Oliver's Yard, 55 City Road
London EC1Y 1SP, United Kingdom

SAGE Publications Asia-Pacific Pte Ltd
3 Church Street
#10-04 Samsung Hub
Singapore 049483

Published by Vivek Mehra for SAGE Publications India Pvt Ltd, typeset in 10/16 pt Georgia by Fidus Design Pvt. Ltd., Chandigarh.

Library of Congress Cataloging-in-Publication Data
Names: Kapal, Rishi, author.
Title: Kites in a hurricane : startups from cradle to fame / Rishi Kapal.
Description: Thousand Oaks : SAGE Publications India Pvt Ltd, [2018]
Identifiers: LCCN 2018033751 (print) | LCCN 2018036274 (ebook) | ISBN 9789352807901 (Web PDF) | ISBN 9789352807918 (E pub 2.0) | ISBN 9789352807895 (print pb))
Subjects: LCSH: New business enterprises. | New business enterprises—Finance. | Strategic planning.
Classification: LCC HD62.5 (ebook) | LCC HD62.5 .K347 2018 (print) | DDC 658.1/1—dc23
LC record available at https://lccn.loc.gov/2018033751

ISBN: 978-93-528-0789-5 (PB)

SAGE Team: Manisha Mathews, Apoorva Mathur, Kumar Indra Mishra and Rajinder Kaur

I dedicate this book to the startup founders, whose impressive advancements, despite hurricanes on the way, inspired me to believe that I was capable of authoring a book to capture their journeys. These people had the courage to bring in the dragons of challenges and eventually tamed them. The world might be nightmarish, but we rejoice and cherish, as competition will perish.

Thank you for choosing a SAGE product!
If you have any comment, observation or feedback,
I would like to personally hear from you.

Please write to me at **contactceo@sagepub.in**

Vivek Mehra, Managing Director and CEO, SAGE India.

Bulk Sales

SAGE India offers special discounts
for purchase of books in bulk.
We also make available special imprints
and excerpts from our books on demand.

For orders and enquiries, write to us at

Marketing Department
SAGE Publications India Pvt Ltd
B1/I-1, Mohan Cooperative Industrial Area
Mathura Road, Post Bag 7
New Delhi 110044, India

E-mail us at **marketing@sagepub.in**

Get to know more about SAGE

Be invited to SAGE events, get on our mailing list.
Write today to **marketing@sagepub.in**

This book is also available as an e-book.

Contents

Foreword

Startups and their world have captured everyone's imagination. The success that many entrepreneurs have achieved has truly been inspiring. Their journeys are laden with struggles yet the fruits are very sweet. It is not only the success that is gratifying but also the journey and the whole experience of creating something from the scratch.

Rishi in his alluringly titled book *Kites in a Hurricane* has beautifully put together a recipe for successful startups. Like Rishi says, "it is a story of how kites (startups) kept flying in a hurricane of competition, with strings of passion and hope." Given his deep association with several startups through his accelerator company, EDUGILD, he is in a unique position to share the knowledge of successes, failures, hits and misses in the exceptional journeys of a variety of Indian startups such as ClassBoat, Simulanis, etc. It is not important to make mistakes and learn every time, one can also learn well from other's mistakes. So also, can one learn from successes of others. Rishi has covered the entire journey of startups in a fascinating manner. He stresses on some aspects that he found common among all the startups he worked with, one of the chief ones being the passion or the belief of the founder in the product or service. He also talks about how all of them start with an almost impossible mission or vision and how relentlessly they chase it and make it a reality.

Entrepreneurship is especially required in my field of work of India–Japan relations as it's all about realizing a hitherto untapped potential. I share my feeling with Rishi in the adventures and fruits of the path of the entrepreneurship and would like to add that it is neither easy nor about doing something that others are already doing. Based on my own experience of raising funds for Tata Group companies from Japan to now running an India–Japan Partnership Fund and the on-going work on the bullet train in India, I can say that entrepreneurship makes sense only for doing something new that you see a strong need for and are passionate about.

I think all entrepreneurs and to-be entrepreneurs will not only find Rishi's book an interesting read but also discover some unknown gems that will go a long way in their search for success and fame.

Sanjeev Sinha
President, India Japan Partnership Group

Preface

As a former Fortune 500 leader and now an academician managing a global startup accelerator, my quest has always been for newer, better, and, most importantly, relevant content to be shared with the learners of any age and domain. This effort includes numerous interactions with the founders of flagship edtech companies, countless pages of reading, and meeting a lot of company people. The exposure and understanding I got from these interactions helped immensely to form the structure and framework of this book.

Kites in a Hurricane is about "a million plates moving together" with startups at the helm of balancing precisely all of them. There are no compromises on this one because if all gears don't move along in synchrony, something is bound to fall. A far-reaching idea that is made real always needs mass appeal to do well, and this is very difficult to achieve. Getting multiple thumbs up on social media is not the same as generating high revenue and employment opportunities.

The startups, even the ones started by matured founders, require a lot of money on their entrepreneurial journey in terms of development and collaboration with the ecosystem. And, everyone wants to see results in the form of considerable progress. My experience shows that simply recreating products, services, and processes on technology and aping the propositions of the Western world will not assure improved quality, efficiency, or financials for the ventures.

What if the founders, educators, advisors, incubators, and accelerators had access to a book that described how others, who have been in the same situation, have used technology and entrepreneurial systems in an innovative manner to solve the problems they face day after day when aspiring to build great companies? The need of a book reflecting these elements was felt, but could not be found. There are several well-written books available in specific domains; however, what was needed was one comprehensive work with real-life examples and explanations about how to combine all the tools related to a startup enterprise to establish a successful company.

Fortunately, when I asked around, I came across some exceptionally thought-provoking, real-life experience stories from our EDUGILD founders across the world, and few other great companies from different places. I could relate to the founders' experiences of challenges, opportunities, late-night ponderation, success, and innovative uses of technology in the space of education and knowledge management at large. I could find stories from venture partners, mentors, and large edtech companies, who have collectively contributed to *Kites in a Hurricane*. With utmost warmth of my heart, I send this note of gratitude to the founders and venture partners for their contribution. I knew, at the very moment, that these experiences and stories must be shared to help guide the way for others to understand the challenges and options when they work on building a great and diverse enterprise.

"Diversity and inclusion" is an important aspect of the content in this book. Almost 40 percent of the companies I have dealt with have either a woman co-founder or women as core team members. It seems that this is more than the global average of the startups where women play an important role.

I strongly believe that these robust and real-life renderings are the most powerful ways to ensure that the readers align themselves to the elements in the book. It would ensure that they visualize how they themselves could do something similar with a high chance of success. What I relish at the end is that each chapter also has its own voice which converges to a perfect symphony in the book. Because of this uniqueness, the book can be read cover to cover, or the readers can pick any chapter and learn from it, depending on the exact need for information and strategies. I sincerely hope that the more you read the book, the more you find it informative, empowering, and inspiring.

Rishi Kapal

Acknowledgments

I first thought about writing each chapter myself, but quickly real-ized that it was the voices of the wiser which had to be included and which would be the most revealing of the underpinning. I am sure of having revealed the information available with real people in the conduit who were involved with the evolution of companies. I would like to thank the founders of EDUGILD's portfolio comp-anies who took out time to contribute in the book. I extend my sincere gratitude to Marius Westhoff, the Vertical Head of UpGrad; Krishna Kumar, founder of Simplilearn; Sachin Tagra, Head of Capital 18 (Network 18 Group); Jan-Cayo, founder of CodersTrust; Anish Bhuwania, founder of Copods.co; Atishe Chordia, founder of DoodleBlue; Dr Yaki Dayan, founder of EdTech Israel; and Pratik Dattani, MD of EPG London, who graciously agreed to pen down words as their contribution to the book and/or gave permission to use their references and formats to make this book relevant for the target audience. The intent is to share the experiences as well as the lessons learned along the way of the *kites* that take up the *mighty hurricane*.

CHAPTER 1

What Changed the World: An Insider's View of Startups

This book tells the story of how kites (read startups) kept flying high in a hurricane of competition, with strings of passion and hope attached. It aims to let the world know how a handful of entrepreneurs had the faith and confidence to create successful businesses in India. It presents the essence of the entrepreneurial experience of companies that may not be very well known but that have moved from being good to great.

The ultimate success of a startup depends on the drive and passion of the founders of the startup. One can only imagine the numerous late nights, frustration, experimentation, and hard work that materialize an entrepreneurial thought into reality. I have had the fortune of being able to work along with several great venture partners (VPs) and supporters to compile this content for the benefit of self-starters and industries alike. In my view, they come close to being the most talented and passionate professionals, whom I may refer to as *champion entrepreneurs*.

This work will take you on a journey of what the founders of flourishing edtech (education technology) startups have gone through—supported by real-life conversations and case studies shared first hand by their management teams. It does not matter whether you are new to the field of tech developers, an entrepreneur, or may be just someone who wants to know what changed the world and how these startups (now companies) came into existence. By the end of the journey, you will be better aware of the behind-the-scenes concept of entrepreneurship—the way it is beyond dazzling, glamorous stories.

This piece also brings forth thoughts from some of the most high-profile technological investors in the world, who put their faith on the idea, opportunity, and concept of the edtech startups. Undoubtedly, a lot of scattered literature will be available on entrepreneurship. However, this is an interestingly unusual attempt to relate the extraordinary story of a very successful Indian entrepreneurship ecosystem. The founders of many companies will appreciate a source that compiles the best practices and learnings through trial and error, which would help fast track the inception and growth of tech startups.

I have ensured that this book is not categorized as an academic research or for that matter a compilation of theories. It should not be read with a view to "learn entrepreneurship in four weeks" since it is not a ready reckoner. This collaborative effort most certainly is about reality and facts, and it captures insights and mistakes that were made on the path to creating successful edtech ventures. It will also describe the common and indispensable elements that need to be considered when a billion-dollar company has to be created.

The Founder's Role

Of the 500 odd startups that I have come across personally during my research on startups, some shone bright, bubbling with exuberance, but were producing something that no one wanted or cared about. This story introduces new ways to approach building great businesses, which naturally involves rejecting and revisiting different business strategies and principles, while handling the high rate of obsolescence in the field of technology, something which moves at a speed that can give even supersonics a run for its money.

As I sit back, relax, and think about what has been common among the startups I have interfaced with, the one factor that stands out is the startup founders and their traits. These founders always kept pace with the changing times and increasing roles and responsibilities. Had they not been dynamic and responsive, they would not have been able to carry on and stand out. Every startup founder believed that one of the most crucial factors to be considered was that the customer had to believe in the company as a brand, and then came the company offering. Some founders were delegators and some were overbearing. However, their behavior adapted to the business, not the other way round, implying that *founders who work for the business are much more successful than those who want the business to work for them.* The prospect of a customer or an opportunity stimulated them so much that the time or day did not matter, neither did countries or time zones. There was amazing chemistry between them and the businesses they were building.

With little or no experience of owning and running businesses, the founders were like spirited children. I sat through them day and night and understood that *the pace of growth does not necessarily have to match expectations.* Hoping otherwise leads to false commitments and frustration. However, these founders have the distinct characteristic of *focus* in their genes. They never took any short-term measures to earn a quick buck or make a runaway impact. I came across companies that could have made good money in the short term but would have lost on bigger opportunities. Their patience never dried up, because it stemmed from their strong belief in what they were doing. Interestingly, none of them became insomniac or got addicted to vices! Their only drive was to keep the faith and grow through sustained efforts and concentration. All the founders faced the dilemma of realizing immediate gains early or waiting for larger ones in the distant future. However, a gamble once is a gamble forever. Another common characteristic I noticed among all the founders was that *at no point did they lose touch with the consumer.* If they considered reorienting their business models, it was because the customer necessitated it, not because there was a quick buck opportunity ahead.

Compilation of Practices

A fact I learnt while interacting with the companies under reference is that it is assumed (though wrongfully) that successful entrepreneurs do not want to share meaningful information with others. A probable reason why people feel that successful entrepreneurs are inaccessible for advice or support to others is that they are so driven by relentless passion 24×7 that they spend every second of their time trying to better themselves, leading to their unavailability elsewhere. Another possible reason may be that any bit of information, placed in the right context, can potentially shape up a future opportunity and unknowingly breed competition—clearly, the founders would want to leverage every new opportunity to their advantage rather than letting anyone else do it. It is tiring and tedious to start a company and hand over opportunities to someone else. Thus, one can imagine the hardships that come in the way of creating and sustaining a concept to reality.

Here, the concept of *sustenance* is the key—reaching a one-time valuation may be considered an indicator of success, but these companies demonstrate that spectacular success comes from sustained and regular up-scaling of the venture. Let us take the example of Simulanis—a company that specializes in creating learning and development solutions, delivered through augmented reality, virtual reality, and gamification. The founder stuck to three basic principles—I am responsible for convincing the stakeholders about the merits; revenue is what makes companies tick; and recognition is an important part of credibility. The founder ultimately led the company valuation to grow by more than five times in the first year and the revenue too increased fivefold within the year. His turnaround time to respond to a communication is less than four hours, and he can be reached 24×7. In a short span of 12 months of acceleration support, Simulanis is already aspiring to set up offices overseas.

The prevalent ecosystem of businesses and technologies is creating a new crop of organizations that are leveraging telecom and technology to get a head start—the frequency with which these startups drive for valuation may actually be a record of sorts (five times in two quarters). These companies demonstrate a *technology-mobility-monetization DNA*—they rely on cutting-edge technology, use the mobile ecosystem, and create solutions that can be monetized—which is a contemporary way of thinking. With 90 percent of India using mobiles, this segment has become the biggest business opportunity one has witnessed so far in our country. To tap this market, the attempt is to understand how these small screens can win the war for these startups, while the world is attempting to woo India through websites on large screens. The startup companies have demonstrated a steep learning curve in the way they have adapted to the mobile phone domain to offer services that are better, cheaper, and greener. While the founders demonstrated leadership and innovation, they put together a team that ensured world-class execution. Of the 20 odd companies that I have been directly advising, all of them have technology at the core of their solution, which allows them to scale up relentlessly—making technology work more than people.

Venture Life Cycle

Keeping startups at the center of what problems are they solving (and does anyone want that problem to be solved or not), it is worth exploring why the activities of marketing, commerce, education, gaming, etc., have started involving mobiles. My assessment of startups revealed that a lot of founders were attempting to solve problems that did not need a solution. No one wanted those problems to be solved since either they were too minor a problem or the users had already accepted them as a part of their day-to-day life. The solutions to such problems, which are insignificant and/or need not be solved, generally land up to have a lot of investment but no buyer in return. With the coming of the mobile phone, the world seems to have converged and every activity involves one communication screen or the other. The startups' success lies not just in technology tracking but also in scaling up operations and constantly keeping track of consumer behavior and needs to deliver innovative and futuristic products and services. The resulting first-mover advantage inevitably leads to astounding success, which gets supplemented with the shift in sociocultural behavior of the new generation. In subsequent chapters, I will describe the problems faced by the companies and their potential solutions, which made a lot of mobile-led engagements less frustrating and driven by user experience.

What forms the basis of a billion-dollar opportunity? I will now elaborate upon the venture life cycle, which is relevant to this discussion. The life cycle zones share challenges that need to be mitigated in order to create a world-class business model, team, and brand—overall, a company with excellence in everything that they do. The description of the life cycle will broadly align itself to what it meant to be a startup, the kind of mentoring and subject matter expert opinions that supported the causes, institutional partners required for beta testing, and the first onsite application, finally leading to the venture capitalist and investors believing in the path-breaking proposition.

The highs and lows of each company will be different; however, there is a pattern in the steps followed by most of the companies under purview. Mentioned here are the steps followed during the inception of the companies that made a mark, with the basic premise that the company already had a prototype or was working on a *minimum viable/valuable product*. Going forward, each of these steps will be connected to a real-life example on how it was put into practice.

Step 1: Being Bootstrapped

Working on shoestring budgets and still pulling off a great start is about frugality. *Bootstrapping is the art of being conscious that money is hard to get.* However, frugality is a culture and not a one-time practice. Startups have to learn the art of building a business with little or no external capital. Bootstrapping is absolutely necessary in order to turn an idea into a profit-making venture. The founders I talked to were not ambitious about glossy offices to start with and shopped for their office requirements on second-hand online (such as OLX and Quicker, to name a few) and offline markets. Once they had acquired second-hand computers, furniture, utensils, and other utility stuff, they did not hesitate to beg for space from friends and family. This is how they minimized capital expenditure on infrastructure and deployed the capital to build technology and manpower. When they had to collect user feedback, the founders tapped into their own networks rather than hiring interns to carry out primary research.

Step 2: Product and Technology Roadmap

How does one distinguish between a dream and an executable product vision? Wish lists cannot drive companies. To materialize dreams, it is essential to have a roadmap and plan of action in place. How detailed should a product and technology roadmap be? As a fulcrum of success, how can technology be employed to keep the company close to the customer? One must work to counter anticipated competition as much as working to be ahead of the existing ones. A few founders I met made clear quadrant charts of their competition, as it existed then *as well as* a roadmap of who could become their competition in 6/12/18 months' time. When I asked them why they are doing so, the simple answer was:

> There are big names in this business, and in 6–9 months if they enter into what we are doing now, we will have new competition. So, it is about time that we create a product that

is ahead of the anticipated competition and that's what will be exciting to our customers.

Step 3: Organization Development

This is a very crucial yet usually ignored aspect. Startup founders find it hard to create a proper organization structure that lends itself to proper delegation of work and/or to establish the need for business partners, without which the startup cannot grow. Startups work on the principle of talent and flexibility; however, lack of proper organizational development may lead to ad hocism, defeating the purpose. In my interactions with one of the startups in the augmented and virtual reality space, the need to recruit or develop a "second in command" to the founder was identified. However, neither is he getting the time nor the right candidate. As a result, the founder's bandwidth is getting completely choked, slowing him down and hampering new business acquisition. The good part is that he recognizes the need and is relentlessly pursuing the matter.

Step 4: Branding the Business and Marketing Management

Most startup founders do not realize the importance of branding early on. It is important to create a brand identity right from the start and not at a time when it actually should become low priority. The next thing to remember as a *mantra* is *revenue first and funding later*—the earlier startups learn and execute this approach, the better it is for them. Further, I also realized that most of the startup founders did not understand *integrated marketing communications* (IMC). In my discussions, along with other mentors, with *Abroad*

Shiksha about how to market their services, we found that there was something amiss and the pieces were not fitting together. We proposed the strategy to synchronize all the elements of marketing management—print, radio, digital marketing, PR and publicity, events, B2B institutions activation—as a package. Such bundling leads to the optimization of efforts toward the desired impact. What IMC approach to choose from is a dilemma that founders must be able to overcome without incurring much cost. This means a robust understanding of the various business models and the efficiency required in deciding on the model to use. If a customer cannot pay for a startup's services, no one would.

Step 5: Investor Relations

Investor hunting, onboarding, and management of expectations are full-time activities inasmuch as they are essential for the business. Time is value, and startups have to know when they have become worth investing. Otherwise, this is a never-ending loop and an experience one may not want to go through. Very few startups know how and when to approach investors. Effective communication is the key. There are critical steps in investor relations; the first of which is to create the marketing material. The subsequent steps include developing a relevant pitch deck, investor Q&A preparation, and shortlisting investors who will genuinely be interested in the startup's proposition.

Step 6: User Experience and User Interface Design

Most startups may have heard about the concept of design and user experience, but I hardly met anyone who really knew what it meant. Almost 80 percent of the startups were hiring wrong profiles for user interface (UI)/user experience (UX) design, since the company founders themselves did not have much of a clue about this element, its impact, and the competencies required. While putting the product concept in place, it is business-critical to involve UI/UX graphic designers at a strategy level. That is the only way one can save time later in creating a great UI for their product. Otherwise, everything may be ready and optimizing the UI/UX may take a lot of time, hindering timely launch.

Step 7: Public Relations and Media Strategy

Observing the public relations (PR) and media strategy of foreign startups while participating in international events has made me realize that Indian startups do not focus on this component at all. A robust media visibility and PR strategy has to be at the core of a startup's business plan. *You do, you show, and you get more to do.* It is paramount for the domain community to view the founders as thought leaders in their space of operations. Such influence is only possible with a robust PR and media strategy, which may include pushing authored articles to the media.

Step 8: Globalizing the Venture

Why do startups believe they are made for the region or country of origin? This is a myopic approach. If the product and service is relevant elsewhere, one can be sure that there are more consumers elsewhere too. Each startup must have a 24–36-month timeframe for a plan to go beyond the country/region of origin. However, this needs compatible, credible, and trustworthy globally established partnerships. As mentors, my team and I envisage all the startups going global. We have already assisted two startups in the UK, to leverage our network and acquire the necessary business sense. Their 1-week visit to the UK did them enough good than what they could have taken six months to do on their own. Edorble.com and Simulanis are the companies that went on the UK immersion program. Thereafter, based on the startups' appetites, we set up partner relationships in the USA, Israel, China, and Australia. The intent is to open up an overseas exposure window for the startups, twice every year, and ensure that steps toward global scale-ups can be planned effectively.

My entire assessment of the Indian startup ecosystem and startup founders brought out the observation that each step that people like me take with startups has to be toward creating a culture of innovation that is tangible and measurable. This is what Israel has done, where 40,000 people, of its approximately 8 million population, work in the high-tech industry specifically supporting the startups ecosystem. Each stage of the venture life cycle needs a push, course correction, and quick execution. Ensuring that the problem statement is well researched and keeping innovation at the center of solution creation will see to it that India has arrived at the startups ecosystem.

The distinctive characteristics of startup founders of true mettle could easily be understood from their background, the industry they were connected to, and sometimes the educational institutes they were associated with. The jewels in the crown were the founders with perseverance and the commitment to make things happen. If one speaks to the founders of Gradopedia and Ekin Knowledge, one would see pure, unadulterated focus and patience to create something which gets the audience right—especially when the offering is complex to execute, but once the consumers experience it, there is no looking back. The whole startup concept hinges on the founder's judgment, ability to dirty their hands, market knowhow, agility to perform, and capability to learn and be mature and willing to sacrifice. For now, how the various venture stages were executed by the startups shall remain a suspense. The subsequent chapters will elaborate on this.

What's in a Mobile? The Blue Ocean of Opportunities

Every morning, the first thing most people (age, gender, caste, creed no bar) would touch is a screen. Today, the number of mobile phones in the world is more than the global population of human beings. Statistics suggest that we may be having close to 2 billion smartphones on our planet. In India, leveraging the smartphone revolution for edtech is still a blue ocean of opportunities, that is, this space has not yet been fully capitalized while the sector is noticing the rising population of smartphones. The world has already been spending billions of dollars on developing edtech applications on smartphones. The world has been spending billions of dollars on developing smartphone applications and marketing strategies using this medium.

In the wake of these developments, it seems unbelievable that smartphones became available only around a decade ago (in 2007), and it is more striking to note that the word *mobile applications* only appeared in 2008, when Steve Jobs gifted the revolutionary iPhone to the world. These path-breaking milestones are relevant to the startups under reference, since their growth story revolves around technology, data, and devices. Mobile handsets, for all practical purposes, are the smallest powerful computers that can be developed, and their size is shrinking further, with the processing and data management capability advancing with each iteration.

The Fundamentals

To put this entire discussion into the correct perspective, it is worth sharing relevant information about mobile devices, operating systems, and enabling technologies that make the proposition of mobile applications so powerful.

It is important to know and consider seriously that while mobile technology took its time to develop, it thereafter experience a boom. Fundamentally, there were multiple challenges in the way of popularizing mobile technologies, of which the most pertinent one was to make them user friendly. Like man's first step on the moon, a giant leap in the direction of user convenience was the creation and adoption of the graphical user interface (GUI). The next challenge was to transfer data usage and management capabilities from computers to handheld devices. This need brought about the term *high-level operating system* (HLOS), which could support functionalities such as email and web browsing to name a few. While Microsoft's Windows OS became a runaway success in the computer world, Google's Android OS created history in the mobile space. Beginning the late 1990s, mobile phone infrastructure started to mature and stabilize, along with mobile phone prices going steeply southwards. While traditional device manufacturers such as Nokia and Motorola relied on proprietary software, the likes of Samsung boarded the open-system Android bandwagon, and created effective and efficient ways for developers to create and install innovative applications. While Windows continued to dominate the desktop/laptop space, history was about to be made by Google in the mobile space.

The Mobile Goes Mainstream

The iPhone (year 2007) unveiled consumer technology that changed the course of history in mobile communications and applications. Now the power of a full-fledged computer was available in a handheld device that virtually integrated every data technology available on earth, and, coupled with creativity, the product was a pride to own.

Along with path-breaking innovation, the iPhone also introduced a *walled garden (closed platform)* operating system, which became the benchmark of high-quality applications. The digital distribution platform for mobile applications, the *App Store*, became the most user-friendly proposition of its time. Another game-changing innovation introduced by Apple was the touchscreen, which facilitated a bigger screen size. Coupled with a gyroscope and positioning sensors, the iPhone now had no challenger in the market. These factors led to the foundation of a multibillion dollar mobile applications industry.

While the Apple OS (iOS) was having a dream run on mobiles, a worthy competitor had to enter this so far blue ocean. This is when Google's Android OS was born. What was offered as a differentiator to iOS was ubiquitous adoption across devices, and individual developers to the world's largest devices manufacturers having the option to customize and optimize the OS according to their needs and purpose.

The adoption trend with respect to mobiles goes to show that the audience has evolved from being a television-watching generation to being a net-surfing generation—from being couch potatoes sitting behind idiot boxes, desktops, and even laptops to taking their digital life on the go—but with time-, money-, and effort-saving applications and content. Mobility and computing in every hand is where the opportunity lies, specifically with respect to mobile applications.

The extent of Internet penetration and adoption has given rise to overwhelming possibilities and already contributed significantly to the GDP of various countries. India is now the second largest Internet user, next only to China and one of the largest consumers of online content through text, audio, and video. If this trend is anything to go by, by 2020, mobile phones and tablets may become the only Internet access devices, implying that anywhere access will not be a luxury but an essential commodity.

The shift toward using mobile applications is gaining momentum due to the competitive prices of the devices and the improved mobile broadband networks. It seems highly probable that most of the next generation will bypass laptops and directly go to mobiles as the first device for Internet access.

Millions of Customers: Billions of Dollars

Smartphones are equated to intelligence, and, for tech startups that are looking to acquire business, they signify effective penetration of technology and thus opportunity. People do not always acquire smartphones because they want to use them, but because they would like to flaunt them. In order to use this channel effectively, it is important to estimate and investigate exactly what smartphones are used for.

Typically, a person may check his/her smartphone approximately 3–4 times an hour. While this may be hard to believe, the number will look realistic if we observe our own engagement pattern and behavior with our smartphones. One can then calculate the number of times an average person checks his phone during waking hours. There is enough evidence to show that smartphones and associated mobile applications are here to stay. The applications are benefiting the entire mobile communications ecosystem—consumer engagement is generating billions of dollars through millions of customers. While the pace of innovation is reducing over time, the opportunities to generate revenue are increasing manifold. Initially, OS providers earned revenue by selling applications through paid application stores. While the applications are created by developers and used by mobile phone users, the OS providers, telecom service providers, and device manufacturers act as aggregators and earn money by just being mediums of application discovery and distribution. This phenomenon has completely skewed the revenue share unfavorably for application developers. This is because the customer is owned by any of the three ecosystem partners mentioned.

In-app purchases and e-commerce associations via mobile applications are a huge revenue generator. Successfully executing an advertising strategy augments the model of an e-commerce channel and is domain-agnostic—edtech, fintech, agritech, whatever the startup may be targeting. Mobile application developing organizations, which have a financial goal to achieve, actually create customers aggressively out of active users through advertising.

Some clear trends are emerging in the universe of applications. It is a fact that a lot of activities are moving from desktops/laptops to mobiles, be it communication, infotainment, gaming, or online shopping. This behavioral shift is just the cusp of transition—an opportunity that was foreseen well in advance by startups that make a difference. The startups have been ahead of consumer needs by tracking user experience.

In the year 2013, it became a common and acceptable notion that the demand for PCs will continue to decline, which was evident from 6–7 quarters of continuously decreasing demand. This was happening because mobile (smart) phones had started to have an impact on people's lives at practically every step. In order to gauge the impact of mobile applications, it is important to understand the influence smartphones have had on the consumers' emotions and psychology. A study on emotional behaviors elicited by smartphones[1] has revealed that social and communicational activities on smartphones have an almost addictive effect on people, which is evident by the Index of Consumer Sentiments (ICS). This seems to be a result of the fact that mobiles, being so accessible and extremely personal, have tremendously increased convenience.

Mobile applications that have been created by the startups capitalize on the concept of "emotional bonding" between a smartphone and the consumer. This proves that success in this realm has not been random; it has been the application of behavioral science. This involves exceptional emphasis on the UI, scalability, performance, and design aspects of the applications. The more an application (app) offers customized connectivity and content innovation to keep the consumer engaged, the more popular the application becomes.

---

[1] van Deursen, Alexander J. A. M., Colin L. Bolle, Sabrina M. Hegner, and Piet A. M. Kommers, "Modeling Habitual and Addictive Smartphone Behavior: The Role of Smartphone Usage Types, Emotional Intelligence, Social Stress, Self-Regulation, Age, and Gender," *Computers in Human Behavior* 45 (2015): 411–20.

There is evidence to prove that people lose patience if they cannot see their phones around, and most people take their phones to bed, leading many to believe that this is a sign of smartphone/digital addiction. Nevertheless, consumer behavior is the reason why business opportunities arise, and, in the context of the present discussion, it is clear that *smartphone penetration is a wonderful opportunity that has changed the world for startups.*

"Apps" Is the Buzzword

While consumers are interested in the convenience provided by an "app", they are indifferent to the protocols used and technology involved in and the intricacies of developing the front end, intermediary, and back end of the app. In order to appreciate the apps universe, it is crucial to comprehend a layman's approach to understanding technology, especially when this universe is evolving faster than the speed of light. What keeps the complexity unexposed to novices and expert users alike is the value delivered by the application and the rich and intuitive UI. Who wants to know the technology being used at the back end as long as the utility to the user makes its mark. Have we ever asked a telecom service provider about the brand of telecom gear they have deployed? It may be reasonable to claim that the simpler the interface, the more advanced and complicated is the software development side.

Now, although an application might be easily ported to an app store, to maximize discovery and downloads, customer engagement is the key. Launching a startup app and gaining web presence is one part; however, being discovered by customers is a different ball game altogether. This is the point at which PR strategies come into picture. Creating the best-in-class products and services is not enough if they do not gain traction, and traction needs experience first and for which the customer must know where to find you. By understanding and digging deep into how startups build billion-dollar apps, chances are that, as a reader, you may want to know the very powerful core of application development and, some day, create an equally compelling application that would change lives and become money in the bank.

Technically, what we call an app is actually a software program, created through a complex process for ease of use. The process is complex because it comes with enormous challenges such as compatibility with multiple mobile browsers and their ever-changing versions and maintaining the user-expected responsiveness at the same time. One cannot imagine how many testing and cutover/fallback procedures are involved when mobile apps have to be launched commercially. As an illustration, I outline here the criteria an application launch by one of the startups needed to meet in order to hit the bull's eye:

- *Performance:* "Oh sorry! We have an error." Simply cannot happen when an app is live with a consumer. Performance of an app means 100 percent uptime and adaptability to any OS, screen shape, size, and type. It is important to ensure that app performance does not vary significantly on different browsers and operating systems.

- *Experience:* It is very difficult to measure the impact and implications of user experience. Ideally, an app must accomplish what it set out to do as well as put a smile on the consumer's face owing to the convenience it offers.

- *Commercialization:* Receiving and delivering services (and money) through mobile apps is a complicated task of integration, which involves regulatory requirements. The value of the service and ease of exchange offered by a mobile app motivates users to increase their share of wallet and volume of transactions through that app.

- *Analytics:* With scores of transactions come gigabytes of data. Now what did the founders do? They did not keep the data in cold storage, but, in fact, used it for analyzing the trend and aligning strategies, leading to a reduction in the cost of customer acquisition (the lower, the better).

The Future Says, "Now You See Me"

There is an increasing clash of opinions on whether we adapt to the way technology is or is technology now adapting to the way we live. The arrival and evolution of mobile broadband, artificial intelligence, and augmented reality are taking future possibilities to unprecedented levels.

Every market that the startups (we worked with) addressed presented an unexplored opportunity, which was identified and leveraged by the companies, thereby gaining a first-mover advantages—blue oceans, which are fast turning red (signifying increasing competition in that space). Mobile technology is evolving rapidly, and to keep pace with it requires a strong foundation, laid by affordable and computationally robust smartphones with ever-shrinking sizes and powerful services ranging from GPS to artificial intelligence. It is unbelievable that predictive and descriptive analyzes of consumer needs and wants can easily be done, making technology anticipative of, and not reactive to, their requirements. Such analyzes have also inspired diversification, whereby wearable gadgets such as wristwatches are also mobile

OS enabled (popularly known as smartwatches). This implies that the consumer is willing to be app-interactive on any device or through any medium. Machine-to-machine integrators and sensors have made the applications more productive and user-friendly, something that will increasingly make apps an indispensable part of our lives. The influence of smartphone functionality on sectors such as education, health care, governance, and commerce is not just here to stay but also to expand by leaps and bounds.

Ultimately, the use of mobile applications needs a secure and stable Internet connection. Here is the challenge India faces in this context: The wireless data technologies such as GPRS and EDGE are consumer saturated, the 3G technology is fragmented and patchy, and the 4G spectrum is inefficient. This is a domain where regulatory framework and influence can make or break mobile-based services. While several startups were attempting to target the bottom of the pyramid, the availability of data speeds and affordability came in the way, and it still does. Claiming to have incorporated 4G technology does not mean one can presume a seamless experience across the nation.

Once the next-generation technology cycle begins, the traditional challenges concerning the Internet, affordable devices, and high-speed processors would have been taken care of. In this era, the shapes and structures of consumer equipment will be more wearable and flexible. Disruptive technology will gain visibility and popularity. The true age of virtual reality will probably dawn—more than 30 percent of the startups are already attempting products and services in the spaces of augmented reality, virtual reality, 3D, gamification, artificial intelligence, natural language processing, and bots (a software application that runs automated tasks) to name a few.

The more you read of the present work, the easier it will be for you to appreciate how opportunity and capability balance themselves to create and recreate history. The Indian startup ecosystem is beginning to distinguish itself in the world of building, scaling, sustaining, and growing a billion-dollar tech-based organization. This atmosphere has the potential to influence and change mindsets, motivate entrepreneurs, instill faith in digital marketing, and make believe that startups will have impact on more than a billion lives. *India has arrived.*

CHAPTER 2

The Difficulty of Being a Good Idea

Of the 300 odd startups that approach me every year for evaluation, there are quite a good number whose idea to create a startup originates from the fact that they have faced some challenges with a product or service. Hence, the founders decide to convert their own problem statement into a solution for the world. To them, I simply ask one question: Have you got the idea validated? Next, if you have identified a problem, do you think people want it to be solved? If yes, are they willing to pay for it? Generally, the conversation goes silent after these statements. The ones that survive such a discussion are the ones that know exactly what they are getting into. It is quite a challenge to determine the basis on which a startup company may be built.

An important aim of this book is to familiarize readers with the relentless hard work and hurdle management done by the founders and their teams, with a never-say-die attitude, and the never-ending belief in the ability to create a compelling proposition. Understanding how startups overcome the challenge of identifying an opportunity from among a million ideas will encourage others to think big, more importantly, in a structured and realistic way. The tasks of raising funds and spending them may appear to be easy, but appreciating how hard it is to put a plan together and execute it to generate revenue is the key to being confident about a "big idea". The experiences that the startups went through will be a guiding light on how real thinking happens at a huge scale.

One thing that never ceases to amaze me is how every startup I have worked with begins with a nearly impossible vision and achieves it despite all odds. I still remember how the founders of ClassBoat and I used to sit at the end of the day, and they would have a glow on their face: "Hey do you know, we collected three more cheques today and two of our earlier users have agreed to renew their business with us." It is important to realize that eureka moments do not come every day. So, when the moment of breakthrough does come, it is important for one to be prepared to give it their best shot and not let the moment pass.

There are many examples of how technology and product startups have impacted millions of users, and they all have a common basis—identifying the need correctly and delivering a meaningful solution to fulfill the need. Every successful company I crossed paths with remained focused on the main idea while always being open to diversifying and scaling to higher levels. However, this is easier said than done. It is a nail-biting experience to go through all the ideas a hunch may generate, and ultimately settle on one that must be focused on to develop it further. Moreover, there is always the risk that the idea that appeals to you the most may have already been taken up by someone else to create a product/service—a fact that may come to light just when you are ready to take the plunge as an entrepreneur.

Did They Know What Was Needed?

We live in a world that is diversified by socioeconomic parameters, demography, language, and behavior. This diversification gets multiplied and more complicated in the sociopolitical and geographical contexts. Startup companies face the challenge of handling the diversity of values, systems of education, ethics, division of labor, usage patterns, housing, hygiene, gifting, rights, perceptions, etc. The founders who understood this well were able to identify the right opportunities. With so many variables at play, it becomes extremely challenging to contemplate and develop an idea that will create a universal problem-solving solution. To be able to address each of these elements while formulating the solution, a clear checklist is needed. *Assessing the implications of each of the aforesaid elements needs exhaustive research till one has adequate information.*

During the first round of startup evaluations, I came across a couple who had just shifted to Pune from abroad with the world at their feet. They had growing up kids, had lived in 12 different countries and had plenty of money and a good reputation when they decided to start a new venture and come back to India. This is a real story of two amazing startup founders. They had to take a quantum leap and understand how their life and finances would be affected when they tried to convert their idea into an opportunity.

When we sat down to do some soul-searching, this is what we found out: Their professional lives had taken them places and made them meet a lot of people, which brought about challenges off and on. However, a common denominator was missing among all the transitions, something they kept realizing over and over again. Then they started observing around themselves and suspected that other people are also affected by the lack of this particular service—the idea they converted into an opportunity later on. While the thought intrigued them every now and then, they carried on with their lives.

However, one fine day, the feelings resurfaced strongly and the thought of taking some action started haunting them. During their sleep, they would mumble about what they wanted to do; their passion for the idea was overpowering them. They set about to figure out the external factors that were to be considered in order to arrive at the solution to the problem at hand (this applies generically to any problem; hence, the name of the company and its services do not need to be specifically mentioned).

This analysis involved talking to hundreds of people across nations, and then a deep dive into the world around: Is the problem genuine and widespread? Are there any political impediments? Will a solution be on the right side of the law or can there be any potential breaches? Will the founders' financial condition allow them what it takes to create the solution? Will the solution have takers who will be willing to pay for the service? Do the founders understand what technology will be needed to implement the service and scale it up in the long term? They also wondered whether the idea was good enough to be translated into an opportunity and should the solution be positioned as a *must have* high-recall brand or as a *good to have* low-recall one. Another important consideration was the geography or place to start with as well as its sociocultural aspects.

Creating a service that does not use a typical social media platform and does not rely on ease of sharing (e.g., Facebook, Instagram) is like reinventing the wheel. In such a case, a startup's biggest hurdle would probably be to capture the customers' attention in a world where nothing is private, and social is the way of life. It sure would be a definite issue to capture attention, be innovative, generate desire and interest, and be disruptive. An average user has hundreds of interactions with their mobile phone every day, which includes messaging, voice calls, checking the time, listening to music, gaming, social media and networking, using the camera, web browsing, scheduling, and charging the phone. This sort of interaction exceeds the human-to-human interaction that happens in a day by an average individual. *This means that the mobile phone offers immense potential to grab a lot of eyeballs on a daily basis.* However, the question is how and why would the target group bother about the company's messages among a huge number of personal and other messages on social media, and then act on it as well. The challenge then is how to adopt the simplest form of communication that can be understood by the masses and classes alike.

There is a common perception that making something cheaper, better, and greener is a sure way of entrepreneurial success. However, the one aspect that the startups I interacted with struggled with was how not to create a solution with just a marginal impact but to launch a service that would change the world for many. Small enhancements and improvements or copying international services and launching them locally may be viable but do not produce the *wow factor*. An idea that strikes a chord with the consumer and creates a subconscious wow is what rises to the top and starts to stand out.

There is so much variability in assessing the right idea fit because everyone tries to be unique in their own way. The general importance of the assessing factors affecting an idea will vary depending on the type of solution one is trying to create. For example, a company creating pesticide-filled dispensers controlled through the IoT (Internet of things) may have to pay more attention to the legal and environmental factors, and a company catering to education loans with automated assessment of eligibility will need to be on the right side of the political and economic laws such as interest rates and RBI and SEBI guidelines.

Wow Moment

Our safari through the wild jungle of startups has thrown up some common observations on the early *wow* moments faced by founders. It is the moment for the founders when they are able to establish that the users will benefit from using the perceived service/product if launched by the company. It is also the moment when the founders are convinced that the potential users will support their solutions and eventually buy them. A heave of sigh at having taken the decision to leave cushy lives and plunge into making ideas come to life is the *true wow moment* that the startup founders talked about. With the first wow moment out of the way, the next challenge for the founders is to create a tornado moment.

Moving on, the idea-to-opportunity journey becomes more challenging with evolving technology, the need to build new platforms, backward and forward integrations of what was done with what is being done, anticipating what needs to be done, and doing so at the right time. It would be intriguing for the readers to know that startup founders gain and lose hope regularly, and the successful ones ultimately come out as shining stars. What matters is perseverance and listening to the right advice; however, *optimal execution remains the masterstroke.* Any preparation is only as good as what actually gets executed; otherwise, it is too little too late. Every bit of effort has associated with it a mix of luck and the risk of losing a handsome, unrecoverable opportunity cost. For the creators of startups, it is the opportunity to lead a good ongoing life, not upsetting the applecart, family considerations, and whatever the world may say. A high-impact event will always have a low probability of making it to the stage early on—what gives high returns is ultimately the uniqueness of the opportunity and the complexity of efforts required to realize the opportunity. Developing a tailored approach may entail designing everything from scratch, but, in the end, it all becomes worth it.

The challenges faced by startups—from idea generation to easy understandability by the consumer—are far beyond contemplation. Every startup's vision is clear that the disruptive approach must have long-term meaning, value, and problem-solving functionality. Perseverance and skepticism go hand in hand. Founders who persevere longer in the wake of skepticism and, most importantly, keep on attempting to enhance their chances of achieving success, adopting the new-generation mobile technology with open arms, always create path-breaking companies—making their offerings essential commodities rather than products or services of aspiration that can reach only a few.

Hurdle Hopping: A Difficult Journey

It is a no-brainer to know that founders' journeys have their own troughs and depressions. There are no prizes for guessing how difficult the process of building a technology startup is, that too relying on universal mobile applications. It is a fact that less than 0.5 percent of funded startups hit the billion-dollar mark; the numbers for India are more dismal, although improving by the day. Considering the past five years, this translates into

1 in 2,000 funded companies reaching the desired heights in a year. There are also compelling evidences of companies growing fast but losing momentum on the way. Making a good idea move into the zone of an opportunity is nerve-wracking, that is, if you are willing to really translate that one great idea into an effective solution for the problem at hand. Every reorientation done by Simulanis, Gradopedia, or StudyMarvel is evidence that the hunt for a great opportunity needs the ideas to be chiseled regularly until a market fit is reached.

Having settled their thoughts on a good idea, the founders struggled through the early stages, and started to see a silver lining just before they were about to lose hope, which increased the likelihood of success—that is when they learnt the lesson that says *patience pays*. It is said that it takes a startup an average of seven years to really become and behave like a company. However, I have seen founders in high-tech domains who worked 24×7 and 365 days a year, reducing the average of seven years to less than half. How? They hunted for ecosystem enablers rather than creating one; they became brands as founders before delegating to the next level; they had a solid roadmap for the future and did not hesitate to say no to short-term benefits.

Perseverance has ensured that these ahead-of-time companies kept together a solid team, earning investors' confidence, building a successful product step-by-step and maintaining *sustainable and strong relationships*. It is also worth contemplating if the early failures of a few startups had anything to do with not having a core team in place. It took them a year to figure out that talent identification, hiring, and doing so at the right time is critical for the idea to germinate into a solution. It is like people taking turns to water a seed so that it can become a tree. Hence, the founders were advised to ensure they hire as soon as there is a hint that a resource is needed. The startups always remembered that companies that evolve from a history of difficulties ultimately always respect human relations, and hence they work on their ideas while staffing the right people and building appropriate work cultures. They do not measure business success only by financial numbers, sometimes the count of smiles and sparks in the eyes also matter.

Since the standards of technology and innovations change the benchmarks continuously, startups need to attract the best human resource available and institutionalize a robust business model linked to dividends. Almost 30–40 percent companies that I was interacting with had women co-founders, and the rapport they shared with their core team members was so amazing that it was a delight to witness their journey.

An entrepreneurial learning curve might be marred with failures and this becomes an eye-opener for external and internal stakeholders. Failures in the case of our founders were instrumental in leading them back to the drawing board with a stronger belief in the proposition. However, they never lost touch with the market. One may conclude that failure leads to substantial learning, since it was important for the founders to acknowledge when they made mistakes or failed, and keep trying until they got it right. However, the question is whether the failure is of the concept/business or it is a personal failure owing to the depletion in social capital. There are emotional situations where founders have a tendency to start blaming themselves for the road-blocking experiences. However, they need to realize that a breakthrough is always possible; one just needs to be patient.

The early failures with some startups could have been due to bad timing, being ahead of time or simply bad luck. Say, for example, a year ago when someone said that my startup is in the area of augmented reality/virtual reality (AR/VR), people used to stay away from them since the ecosystem itself did not understand what it meant to be in AR/VR. However, times have changed and today startups based on AR, gamification, 3D, VR, artificial intelligence (AI) and non-linear programming (NLP) make up more than 30 percent of the companies I have engaged with.

The difficulty of being a good idea also stems from the fact that while you know your competition today, what matters is who do you expect as competition in the future. You may beat the existing ones today but someone may come out of the blue in the future, so your idea and the solution have to be *futureproof* more than *featureproof*. One of the founders was like a periscope in a submarine: When the rest of the team were diving deeper and deeper into the problem, this one had their neck out at all times—scanning the environment, picking up clues on consumer behavior, and sniffing new opportunities, ecosystem enablers, and competition. The founders remark that they always ensured forward-looking vision by being constantly responsive to the changes in the surroundings; that way they kept themselves closer to the market and adaptive to the changes around. One of the founders I spent time with was upfront to say:

> We thought our gut feel about an idea was all that was needed to create a venture. Whatever ecosystem we interfaced with told us not to go for a hardware-based solution as it has long-term cost implications, but now we are stuck with a short-term ideation view. Rather than focusing on building up we are struggling to figure out what to do with the product at hand.

Traction Development Difficulties

There is evidence to suggest that aspiring to become a large company brings about a common set of difficulties. Scraping through those difficulties is something that made a few Indian startups what they are today. Here are a few parameters/characteristics of the typical difficulties and challenges that often confronted the companies.

- *Long haul:* Startups do not succeed overnight, and no high-value tech company has met with immediate success (exceptions should never be confused for a general rule). Whether it is for expansion, initial public offering (IPO) or acquisition, a period of 7–10 years is normal. The perseverance demonstrated by the founders becomes the key to making their path smoother.

- *Business model:* Selection of a business model is a difficult proposition for companies to undertake as an activity. At the end, a business model is as good as the business it can generate and impact. This activity involves contemplations and discussions around successful online services to offer such as gaming, e-commerce, and SaaS (software as a service) or simply becoming a cloud solution provider, a B2B or rather B2C company. B2C is the way to go, along with the new concept abbreviated O2O (online to offline and offline to online). During a snacks session with one of the company founders, we asked him why he was going and conducing classroom seminars while his model was to create an edtech venture, to which he simply stated, "I will generate awareness offline and then move them online." Little did he realize that sometimes classroom/physical interactions become addictive and restrictive at the same time. He started spending so much time offline that his attention to tech-based solutions started becoming an issue. His original idea was now languishing. What lacked here was *focus*; and the moment the focus was back, the idea was revived: It became an opportunity. The challenge of delivering something unique and creating a business model to implement the opportunity has made many founders go through the learning curve leaving egos behind—age is no criterion to determine the need for learning something.

- *Exposure:* The challenge of experience and seasoned exposure to category and technology became a hurdle to be crossed by the founders. It is important for the founders to rely on the combination of passion and experience of the community around them to ensure that technology as well as business exposure increase the chances of the venture being successful in the first attempt. However, too slow an exposure can be quite painful. We have seen founders who have the compulsive disorder of ensuring precision sometimes lose on opportunity to someone who prefers efficiency over precision. Remember, it is *swiftness now and precision forever.* Never reverse this equation.

- *Advantage education:* What challenges can be mitigated with the founders being exposed to a tech ecosystem early? Simple ... it can reduce the idea's time to market. Tech companies need founders who understand enough so as to not be taken for a ride by anyone else.

- *Geography:* It is said that you start with a disadvantage if your company is instituted in India. Being an India-based setup sometimes becomes a challenge in terms of the support that can be had in terms of institutional and technology access. India does not lack anything, it is just that the founders do not get what they need on a single platform. While this may be a fact at present, it also seems very possible that the global and Indian horizons are going to cross paths very soon.

Startups are surviving and overcoming these challenges thanks to their determination to reach the goal—their companies are life force for them—that is all they need to survive. The next challenge is to combine all the aforementioned efforts with a team that believes in maximizing potential to create brands rather than getting lost in the existing ones.

Founding Team, Validating Beta, Seed Funding

Let us reemphasize the first few steps in reaching the initial milestones of a successful proposition.

- *Idea vs opportunity:* It is not certain whether every idea is an opportunity unless and until it is validated, tested, and the feedback incorporated. Startups have to go through this first step by putting the idea on paper, taking test market inputs, and refining the proposition based upon feedback over and over again until a critical mass believes that what they are doing is monetizable.
- *First office application (FOA):* It is important for startups to figure out how their proposition would translate into an application so that it has an easy-to-use interface and is communicable to others through word of mouth. Getting the product into the users' hands quickly and gaining mindshare is extremely important during prototyping. FOA is a critical step for idea validation: Would someone in your friends and family help you test your hypothesis and then the prototype? This is

where startups lose most of their time. Once the final product is ready, it has to be followed up with a strong drive toward delivery of the solution, so that it reaches the real users as soon as possible. Investments can only be secured if the associated complications of the solutions are backed by undisputed trial results and proof of concept.

- *Soul mates:* Team members that share the founders' vision and complement their skills are their *soul mates*. This is what made most startups' journeys fun and result oriented. Founders also have to ensure they get people better than themselves on board, so that a winning team could create winning solutions—the founders have too much to handle personally. The startup teams have key roles such as leading the product vision, identifying and using the technology of choice, and most importantly focusing on monetizing the concept and getting customers on board.

- *Beneficiaries:* The ultimate beneficiary of the solution has to be the consumer (along with the investors if they are already a part of the system). However, the network of friends and family members must use the created solution before commercial launch and be brutally honest in giving feedback, both good and bad. The next step is to identify the target group and ensure that mass feedback is also incorporated for improvements.

- *Go-to-market (GTM) model:* It is a strength as well as a challenge for startups to have a GTM model in place, right from the initial days itself, something that is generally untested and more hunch/instinct/gut feel oriented. The challenge is to ensure a robust data analytics platform from day one, which provides information on user behavior and thereby keeps having a constructive impact on business performance as soon as the prototypes are out on the FOAs.

Getting all these steps right ultimately leads to the bigwig investors taking notice and making valuable investments.

Appetite for Constructive Disruption

The journey of most startups begins with the simple question: How much are the founders and associated teams willing to sacrifice with success in mind? Success, they say, is counted sweetest by those who have never achieved it, those for whom it came close but remained out of reach. This way, it always remains an aspiration. Success may be the result of going through hundred hours a week of work, conflicts and depressing market feedback, people refusing to believe that they can have a career with the company, or the legal, regulatory hassles standing as showstoppers. To top it up, come the nightmarish efforts of chasing investment to ensure that the idea remains novel and alive. Such are the tough calls to take along with treading the thin line between how much to tell and how much not to the network of people around, since someone may pick up the idea and become an immediate competition. Perseverance and sacrifice are the pillars upon which the founders create strong company foundations. They do not escape the sweat, fear, and facing failure upfront, but definitely overcome them.

Sometimes, new companies struggle to realize that entrepreneurship must be monetized. This calls for efforts toward deeper understanding of potential business models. Non-paying customers may be sustained due to the charm of numbers, but then the cost of an idea sometimes becomes too prohibitive to afford. While there are the successful billion-dollar models of WhatsApp, Candy Crush, and Clash of Clans, the founders had the task of converting challenges into opportunities and becoming Indian names to reckon with internationally. Gone are the days when speculative business models sold and the transition from freemium to premium was not needed. Providing services for free is neither a science nor an art; eventually, lack of revenue generation just means allowing bargaining powers to customers and suppliers alike (Porter's five forces model coming alive, a great framework to refer to for startups businesses). Every solution that the customer likes has to be reciprocated with their willingness to pay for it. Charity sells but does not deliver anything. Monetization of an idea entails the challenge of keeping the costs to such an optimum level that they would be always less than the revenue generated, potentially.

No business achieves perfection from day one. However, keeping the customer at the epicenter and creating something viable leads businesses to achievements. Since today's business world has become one of low barriers to entry, it is imperative for founders to perfect their business model very early.

An improved business model needs refinement, which improves the company's ability to attract investors early on. This step would not have been the ultimate aim for the organization; however, it helps to expedite the realization of the ambition to build a sustainable business model. All the initial decisions one way or the other create a snowball effect and become the core of the business in the future. The process discipline of putting together the best research, hiring employees better than the founders, formulating a workable business model, and convincing investors about the potential of the idea lays the foundation to overcome the difficulties encountered in creating opportunities out of an idea.

Converting an idea into an opportunity is like giving birth to a child, just that the time of the transition is unpredictable. It is *you* and only *you* responsible for the fate and future of your startup regardless of the circumstances. *No one will ever be as passionate about your idea as you will be.*

CHAPTER 3

Face in the Dark

A gutsy stroke of wind came down
Someone heard a shout
As silence took over everything
And blew the lantern out...

You may have read these lines...

Simply put, it is important to understand the criticality of *becoming a brand* early enough in the life cycle of a startup, which becomes a strong entry barrier for competition. The problem is that while attempting to create world-class products and services, most startup founders tend to overlook thinking about how their business can become a brand.

I have asked many startup founders this: Tell me when will you call yourself a brand? Or in other words, why do you associate any product or company with a brand? Most of the founders reply by saying that as their businesses are in their initial years, they cannot claim to be a brand. However, I always tell them that the age of a business has no correlation with its branding. *Wisdom*, which is independent of age, is the key; that is exactly what matters.

As a business, when you live up to the promise you make to the customers and continue doing so again and again, you become a *brand*. The promise can be of quality, speed, price, innovation, packaging, ease of use, or whatever feature that matters to the users. In turn, your key propositions develop a strong recall value and there emerges a brand; Fasoos[1] is a good example to align with this definition.

While a zillion of companies get launched and millions of them make money, only a handful go on to become brands. In the absence of a strong focus on branding from the initial days, a majority of the companies become a face in the dark for a while before succumbing to competition sooner than later, who may capture customers' and stakeholders' (investors included) attention by being visible while doing only half of what you may have been doing.

Gathering attention, generating interest, instilling desire, and encouraging action need a compelling name, logo, and brand proposition. These are needed even before one can think of any formal marketing communication. The startup founders I interacted with did not demonstrate the skills to fully understand the essentials and impact of marketing and brand management. Some believed that consultants and agencies will do what it takes, while for others it was low in their priority list. And, this is where the entrepreneurial world is mistaken. The customers to be targeted are exposed to a world of millions of options actively craving for

---

[1] While Frankies and vegetable-stuffed rolls have existed for a long time, people associate Fasoos with food "on the go". In hindsight, what they now serve are stuffed rolls; however, the consistency in their quality, packaging, and customer services has created a strong recall value, which makes Fasoos stand apart as a brand.

their attention and eager to ensnare them. A startup has to have a strong organizational identity to become a true asset, a synonym of trust, and to break away from the rest very early on. Let us not forget that a business needs to earn not just revenue and profit but also recognition, respect, and loyalty from its customers. Branding as a fundamental element plays a huge role, even to the extent that it can pull through a startup about to go bust.

Brand value is an element of profitable consideration as much by investors as for revenue generation. An early attempt to create a brand and its recall is a "hygiene factor" and not optional. My 20 odd years of experience in sales and marketing have taught me one thing: *joh dikhta hai who bikta hai (what is seen is what sells)*. Going forward, in the new startup climate, investors will put their money into a brand only if it looks profitable rather than a brand built on discount sales.

It is near impossible to create a brand that wins mindshare quickly. It is a mammoth task but a very critical one that needs focus from the very early days of the startup. My suggestion for the startups I interacted with was that the founders should settle for a brand name that had consumer appeal and resonance along with retainability and capability of gaining mindshare. The names became relevant since the services were simply defined by the words that constituted a company's identity. Since the brand name reflects the company's personality, the first impression always matters. The value of brands to companies is like that of reputation to people—easily lost but difficult to gain. Customers' first interface with the brand influences how they perceive the service/product (such as, enhanced convenience and reduced cost), which will leave an impression in their minds, to be recalled later just by hearing the name.

To gain further insight into branding, I sought the opinion of successful entrepreneurs in my network and others who had taken professional branding advice. The long and insightful conversations with the startups and branding experts brought out following two key lessons on how to create a meaningful and vibrant brand early in the game:

- *Simple and memorable:* Do not create tongue twisters since the customer is not competing in that activity. Choose a name that is simple and easy to remember and recall.
- *Distinctive to the service:* You cannot call yourself *Jackie's Cove* and deliver AR products. Your service is technology-based and your company name cannot be identified with a restaurant or an adventure trip management company.

Know Your Community

Starting with the right mindset, elaborate discussions brought about the branding vision. Most startup founders I met were very convinced that branding means having a digital marketing agency that will create a logo and then get paid on the one part for nurturing social media and creating followers, and on the other part for answering FAQs and avoiding controversies. Their approach seemed grossly wrong, but they were not to blame, since they were unaware that brand building needed to be the top priority.

I realized that few of the startups not only spent sweat and hours to do their mainstream work but also involved themselves in the local community of social work and engagement, offering their services as volunteers, speakers, judges at events, etc., in an attempt to make themselves visible and available. They attempted to create a snowball effect of attention in the vicinity, which would create immediate positive word of mouth, also increasing the chances of adoption of their products and services initially in their neighborhood itself. The startups were demonstrating the desire to connect with their community and participate in creating and sharing experiences; they used their shared values for a better bargain and seemed to have the potential to leapfrog faster.

The startups also demonstrated a unique trait: speed of capitalizing on an opportunity. I told one of the guys, "Hey, my friend has created a tech platform, you may find it useful." I had just finished the statement and the guy already had his phone out and asked me the number to dial for talking to my friend. The call happened instantly, and the demo was slotted in the next eight hours. Amazing, isn't it? Both sides earned early respect for one another. The same is true for the potential customers as well. More than a service provider, they should see a friend in you: *The first branding of a startup is the founders themselves.*

Our friends creating world-class companies managed to cultivate all the aforementioned qualities, and that is how they got their brands to great heights in a short span of time. They remembered one thing: Always respect another company and its founders. In our ecosystem of startups, we saw almost 50 percent founders identifying synergies with other companies in the network and trying to co-develop businesses. This was possible since the companies had diverse services but the same target audience. This collective approach helped these companies to lower their acquisition costs and hence march faster toward breakeven point.

A Lot in the Name

It would have taken several brainstorming sessions to slightly inebriated conversations involving friends and/or business partners to generate the original idea for the brand to be called

Simulanis and their offering to be called Saral. It was considered critical to use the brand name as the domain and later the app name as well. This was important since the brand interaction with the users directly translated for them to reach out to the web/app for exploring the services. The brand name ensured that the company did not lose its identity in the red ocean and distinctively maintained its presence online as well as offline. Being the owner of a brand and then its associated digital properties such as the website and application was on the lines of owning tangible real estate at a desired location. The objective while selecting the name was to ensure that the brand interacts with the users to develop trust, which would be followed up with the credibility of service. Before the service is used, the most impressionable experience for the customer is the brand, and here starts the valuation.

It is important to understand a few things very clearly, very early. The name of the company must be such that the customer should get a good and clear idea about the company without the need for an elaborate description or presentation. Once the name has been decided, the *naming ceremony* is extremely important to let the outside world know what the company stands for and the kind of genre they represent. Simply put, the company name is a small dynamite that explodes with many but relevant meanings. The companies that I interacted with created brand names and logos, and modified them until they seemed fit to capture the customers' interest.

There was also the realization that passionate founders do not delegate the process of brand naming. Either they get into consumer research themselves, or, if an external agency is engaged, they also involve themselves completely in the naming process, participating in intense brainstorming as and when required. That is how important naming your brand is. It is not something you delegate to a committee or something that gets accomplished in a few brainstorming sessions with your agency. Upon enquiring with the founders, they were clear (and we made them understand the seriousness if they did not already) that naming the brand—be it the organization or the solution on offer—is a decision that can shape the future and scale of one's startup.

Version 1   Version 2   Version 3

Consider the dilemma of the founders of ClassBoat when they were clearly told that their brand identity is stale and does not connect with the target audience. (The magical sort of hat on their first logo was supposed to reflect a boat!) Once it was agreed that the branding has to be more appealing and international, our designers worked relentlessly with the ClassBoat team and brainstormed until the logo and identity were made more engaging. The new identity was run past a focus group, feedback incorporated, and then finalized.

After a company agreed on using a specific identity as the brand and front end/name, the team started putting their minds together on how the logo will look and feel in terms of visibility, color scheme, and display style. These elements put together in the right proportion would lead a brand to be visible in the eyes of the stakeholders.

Brand development for all the proper reasons has a lot of options. During a marathon session on branding and marketing with the founders, we realized very early that UI/UX experts and graphic designers must be an integral part of the brand development process and not external to the cause. Sometimes there were debates and heated arguments about how to finalize a brand/company name/logo. There are unlimited options and sometimes that itself is a problem. Let us think of a typical scenario: Founders sitting with excitement in their eyes but a grim face with uncertainty, and the task at hand is to create their brand name/ identity. In such situations, founders sometimes have eureka moments. So, one gets up and says, "Guys, I have found it: The company name will be a combination of a few alphabets of my name and a few alphabets of my spouse's name. Or better still, let's name the brand as a mix of our kids' names!" Such suggestions have such a strong emotional appeal that, sitting on the other side, it is difficult to gather courage and tell the founders how childish the idea really is.

NOW

Schoolsaamaan.com

THEN

Let's look at an example. Earlier branded as "Schoolsaamaan", the company renamed itself as "YoScholar", which reflected an entity that goes beyond just providing school-related utilities. Its web portal, an e-commerce marketplace for educational products and services, went from being "Schoolsaamaan.com" to "YoScholar.com". The rebranding reflected the company's vision and evolving focus, with students at the center of its strategy.

Schoolsaamaan.com was launched in Bangalore in March 2015 as an e-commerce company. It began with selling products online for school goers, such as uniforms, books, and shoes. Thereafter, it expanded its reach to the NCR and Pune. Simultaneously, it also broadened its offerings to include student accessories, fancy dresses, educational and sports kits, among others. Today it has 60+ sellers empaneled, catering to a large number of students and their parents. With its new identity, YoScholar, it wanted to reaffirm its commitment to be a full service facilitator for students, vendors, and institutions, providing the entire range of necessities, from dressing to learning and development.

Amit Mishra, co-founder of YoScholar, claims that the new name represents and highlights their focus on students as the center of the education ecosystem. In the FY 2016–17, YoScholar has recorded more than ₹5 crore in gross merchandise value (GMV) and partnered with Vedantu, Fundamentor, and ChildAcademy for expanded offerings to schools.

Being open-minded while identifying the company name does not guarantee that you will get it right the first time, especially if the exercise has been done without using logic and rationale. Whether you want the name to describe your work or be something abstract, *it must make sense to the customer*, which is what will drive and grow the company. Usually, the brand names chosen by startups are either acronyms, e.g., Ekin, implying we are your electronic kin, or simply descriptive, e.g., Abroad Shiksha—no sweat—we are your partners for facilitating education overseas, clearly indicating the service being offered by the company.

Descriptive names can straightaway convey the business the company is in, making positioning easier. However, such names can at times be constraining. For example, if a company diversifies or does a forward integration, the name becomes a pitfall. Names may also be abstract yet meaningful. Take ClassBoat, for example—one is looking to decide on a course of study to fulfill one's passion; they get a boat to sail them through the options—the name conveys the message to a large extent. If ClassBoat diversifies further, the name will not come in the way of customer understanding. However, there is a new science in creating company names, which I learnt from a company named Edorble. Many people have misspelt and mispronounced the name but the founders stand by the name they created. Edorble is an "invented name" and again is multidimensional. It is a made-up word and will always represent this one company. Such names do not come with any baggage or competition; if pulled off well and used effectively, supported by a solid branding strategy, these are the most powerful names.

There was one specific issue in branding which I kept encountering with most of the startups—the founders were forgetting to map the competition while creating a brand name. It is worth realizing that competition is not something that needs to be considered only in the context of products and service concepts; they must be considered while branding and naming the company as well. As a start, I have always insisted that the startups map the existing competitive landscape. It begins with creating a list of names/ brands the startup expects to compete with. This can even throw up a pattern in case most companies in the same domain have used the same class of names. Such observations can help the company avoid branding errors.

There are a few important benefits of mapping competition while creating your brand identity. At a glance, it lets you gauge the wall you are up against and how porous it is. Second, it also allows you to assess the battlefield and the opportunities that branding can take advantage of, which otherwise will be identified by competition sooner or later. And brand creation is not a routine activity; it has to be done right the first time. Few of the startups I have been advising for the last one year now realize that their brand name is not reflecting their true identity, and it must be changed sooner or later.

The Domain Name Wrinkle

Once we were nearly settling on the brand name, the key consideration of digital presence came up, starting with the domain name. A key decision in the naming process is to determine whether or not the brand requires a domain name, and, if yes, then do the brand and domain name have to be the same? For example, One97 is known by the brand name Paytm, so there are precedence of different company and domain names as well. If you are naming a company, you can guarantee that a domain name will be required. With a B2B product or service proposition, you may have a bit more leverage and may not need a domain name. However, the requirement of domain name purely depends on how the company wants to market and promote its offering.

Finding an available .com domain name is very hard, unless you are working with invented words. One of the startups I have been advising is in the space of VR-based meditation. Created by Ashwin, who is a monk of 17 years, and Diane, herself a mother, the company has great technology as well as good content for mind, body, and soul programs. While the company named itself "Ahhaa"—a very apt connotation of how its services would make one feel—it became very difficult to own the domain name Ahhaa. com, since it was already registered and owned by someone else.

The company initially settled for Ahhaa.co; however, the magic of .com is always bigger and better. The founders of Ahhaa were faced with two options: either to change the company name to another invented name or to buy out the .com domain. The general thoughts were to change the company name (and many other names were explored as well). However, collectively we could not avoid the stickiness of the word "Ahhaa". Eventually, the founders figured out the owner of Ahhaa.com and made a deal to pay for the domain through EMIs. Now the company domain Ahhaa.com is live, and work is happening on populating it with propositions and engagements for the present and future. The learning we got as a group is that it is good to assume that almost all the relevant domain names have been registered, but that does not mean all of them are being used. If you can convince the existing domain owners, then it is possible to get the domain name you aspire for. However, the earlier one does it, the better it is in order to avoid the brand value leakage.

One must also take care that buying a domain name should be coupled with securing the similar named ones as well. This avoids confusion in case anyone else launches another domain that is similar to yours. For example, there are two companies that are pronounced the same—Flinnt.com and Flint.com—the user can easily confuse between the two. It would be better if either of the founders would lock similar domains and websites.

Moving ahead on the journey, during a meet of 30–40 startup founders, I had posed a simple question to them: Have you allocated a budget to purchase the domain(s), and if yes then how much? Much to my surprise, almost half of them had not thought about the money involved in purchasing and maintaining domain names. While for B2B- or B2B2C-oriented brands, the budget required would be low, for companies aspiring to be totally B2C-oriented, which would engage a larger audience, the budget required to create a domain and effectively grow the brand would be higher.

With this basic logic in place, the next challenge is to create consistency in the brand visibility. To this end, the startups I worked with were asked to work on branding guidelines. It is an important piece of the branding puzzle, since the logo, font, color, placement, aspect ratio, and everything one can think of need to have a process and structure, as the brand/logo will be represented on various collaterals.

The Brand Pre-test

Once the startups had decided on the brand name to go with, I had the daunting task to develop the key performance indicators on which the brand could be pretested before money is spent to launch and promote it. To this end, brainstorming sessions with a few successful companies on one hand and branding experts on the other started, and we collectively put across a few parameters.

- *Say the name:* The startups were asked to clear their minds and slowly keep repeating the brand name. Did it sound easy to say, did it ensure there was no tongue-twisting, was there a positive vibe, did it sound creative?
- *Self-identity:* Did the brand name stand apart from competition? Did it sound cliché or futuristic? Could it accommodate more than what the competition has to offer as of now?
- *Recall:* I went around with the startups and they recited their brand names to a few people in their close social networks.

After 48 hours, we called all these people and asked them if they recalled the brand names. This exercise gave the startups adequate confidence about the stickiness of the names and their representation.

- *Collaterals:* The brand names and symbols were printed on sample stationary material, giveaways, and presentation templates to assess whether they looked as good on print as they sounded when spoken.

The aforementioned judgment calls had to be made taking into account practical aspects more than emotional aspects, which led to the right branding decisions for the startups.

Marketing Management: Integrated Marketing Communications

It is relevant to highlight that digital marketing is only a part of IMC. Startups must evolve a holistic IMC plan and embed digital marketing as an integral element of the same. The mistake committed once too often is that while budgets are unleashed and unproductively spent only on digital leverages, the other IMC elements remain untouched. In such situations, the marketing budget is not utilized to its full potential.

While the world has taken a fancy to digital marketing, once too often my dialogues with the startups led to the conclusion that digital is not their way ahead in the short term. If you are a B2B company, no matter how much digital social activation you may do, it simply dampens out along with the money. IMC is a formal subject, which I used to teach in classrooms earlier and am now guiding startups on.

There are five elements to IMC, and founders have no clue about the landscape:

- Advertising
- Sales promotion
- Personal selling
- PR and publicity
- Direct marketing

For startups at any stage, the key is to choose just the right blend of the IMC elements and present a consistent, seamless, and multidimensional brand image across a range of marketing initiatives.

The thought of mentioning IMC came to me when I was discussing marketing strategies with the startups. The immediate realization was that there is too much marketing noise in the edtech world, and digital seems to mistakenly be considered a savior of sorts. Having said that, none of the startup founders had a way to assess their core marketing needs based on their business and GTM model.

The initial challenge was to understand the immediate needs of the startups and to work out which marketing strategies will work the best for them. So a format was created for each startup to assess their integrated marketing needs and apportion appropriate budgets. The action plan actually started when the discussions were happening with ClassBoat, Abroad Shiksha, and YoScholar. It did not take much time to realize that one marketing tool will simply not cut the ice. For example, with YoScholar, mailers were sent to school principals informing them that the company is an online facilitator of school supplies. There was a lot of euphoria to immediately launch a digital campaign and spend money on email marketing. At this stage, their strategic VP asked them to stop and understand that all school principals (or most of them) are not well-versed with email as a mode of communication. This also set us thinking whether the companies really know about the preferred communication channel and media habits of the consumer/influencer. So, collectively, the founders of YoScholar, their VP, and I agreed to put a multipronged marketing strategy in place since the influencer/decision-maker may need more recall episodes. Eventually, the first burst of emailers went out, followed by physical letters and offer details sent through traditional post, and finally an SMS campaign to ensure there is immediate recall of the services.

In a world with so much marketing noise, my team went a step back with the whole integrated marketing piece and started an assessment process, as captured in the format shown in the Appendix to this chapter.

It is important to understand and be conscious of the fact that a startup's potential customers are someone else's target/potential customers as well. These customers are constantly pinged with various marketing efforts as well as varied content. In such circumstances, the important aspect is to ensure that the company has a holistic understanding of all the marketing tools and techniques. Take Classboat.com for example, initially, while deploying marketing tools and budgets, the assumption was to attract customers through a digital reach. However, it was evident, as we slowly unraveled the marketing focus, that PR and publicity will become their unbeaten weapon. So, with ClassBoat, the work involved placing appropriate marketing information in national media.

One of the lessons learnt while closely working with ClassBoat, Ahhaa.com, YoScholar, and Abroad Shiksha is that it is mandatory to integrate the online and offline world of marketing tools. Today's target audience expects to find their need fulfilling services and products super quick. If they hear or see an advertisement, they would explore the brand's app or website immediately. Since it is a fact that instant access to information must be provided to the audience, so to use traditional marketing without augmenting its recall through latest technology marketing can shrink reach, increase time to reputation, and even position a company as a laggard. It is for this reason that a lot of work is going on with the founders of Abroad Shiksha to get their technology platform up and running: They are being marketed around the country and people expect their solutions to be futuristic.

How Integrated Strategy Was Set Up

Another lesson learnt in the marketing journey with startups was to gain awareness of the media habits of the consumers. In case of Simulanis.com, it was pure B2B marketing, once the company repositioned themselves from being Saral Books to being a strong AR/gamification skills development proposition to corporates. Hence, speakership at events, participation in roadshows, and creating compelling brochures and reading material became the essence of the whole integrated marketing plan—no digital marketing got deployed since the consumers/influencers and decision-makers were not expecting the digital media platforms to be a place for discovering Simulanis' solutions. However, wonders were done by loading real-life Simulanis propositions on YouTube and activating their LinkedIn profile. So, staying focused on the right marketing tools bore the results we all expected for Simulanis. Along with the founders, the steps of the marketing journey that still remain are as follows:

- *Objective of the campaign:* Simulanis is one of the rare Indian startups that went ahead and carved a global strategy. UK was a strategic destination identified for Simulanis and the marketing plan included alignment with the UK companies such as Economic and Policy Group (EPG) and Immerse Education.

- *Deciding on the marketing channels:* In order to initiate Simulanis' engagement with the European ecosystem, our UK partner EPG took Simulanis founder Raman to high-profile edtech events such as EIC and BETT and began introducing him to the UK ecosystem.

- *Devising a social strategy:* Back home, social media—LinkedIn and Twitter—was set abuzz to announce Simulanis' plans of going global and taking support from the Startup India initiative.

- *Planning the required skills and resources:* Raman was running pillar to post for business operations, expansions, as well as investor relations. It was important for him to get hold of a strategic team member in order to execute the vision.

- *Creating and deploying the campaigns:* A campaign is as good as the result it delivers. In the case of Simulanis, the campaign objective was to position them as leaders in the AR/VR space. All the word-of-mouth effort, PR and publicity, promotions, and events were focused on this objective. The activities were done in bursts every quarter so that the focus on business development was not compromised.

Especially when startups are concerned, integrated marketing does not mean using every channel of the five elements around, but only the ones that match the media consumption habits of the users and, hence, are likely to reach the target audience. It is worth mentioning that all marketing tools do not work for all companies; selecting the right ones saves not only money but also a lot of time, while delivering the desired effect. Choosing the right channel for marketing communication is of utmost importance, failing which the entire strategy and execution falters.

Let us discuss another very classic case of IMC for Abroad Shiksha. They operate in the space of ensuring admissions for deserving Indian students in international institutions. The journey with Abroad Shiksha and their VP was to ensure that their technology solution is able to bring about higher transparency in the process as compared to such services delivered by the bricks and mortar service providers in this space. Having said this, the strategy to be deployed for Abroad Shiksha had following multiple elements:

- *B2B:* Visiting academic institutions and conducting seminars.
- *Word of mouth:* Leveraging earlier beneficiaries to bring in new candidates.
- *Advertising:* Campus ambassador programs launched in various institutions in order to gain a foothold.
- *PR and publicity:* Getting Abroad Shiksha visibility in national newspapers such as *The Economic Times* and associating them with specialists in the space of education management.

Abroad Shiksha faced an interesting challenge—the founders were not comfortable making presentations—they confessed to having stage fright. However, they excelled at guiding prospective candidates through the whole admission management process. The B2B part of their marketing involved creating standardized communication templates detailing the company and its offerings, devising social media strategies, and evolving GTM programs. With the US visa situation and Brexit, the year for Abroad Shiksha was looking slightly slow; however, the right marketing tools and focus made them recover lost ground, if any.

Social Media Platforms and Integrated Marketing

Next comes the creative stage. While dealing with the day-to-day tactical and overall strategic elements with the companies, we realized that the marketing communication must align with the overall integrated messaging, adapting traditional as well as online channels. For example, YoScholar may benefit from participation in events and audience presence. ClassBoat may prefer a crowdsourced information model or referrals in order to attract clients, while also employing B2C marketing for the learner to know that the best education solutions can be discovered on ClassBoat. Each marketing channel must convey a concise, relevant, and consistent brand message.

Working with portfolio companies, it becomes imperative to embrace social media as an essential element of an integrated marketing strategy. Social media marketing is not a fad but here to stay. The first step for each startup is to understand the social media landscape and the objectives of using it. Simulanis may use it to showcase their strengths in AR/VR while YoScholar may use it to position themselves as a "peace of mind" company for parents of school-going children. When considering social media, it is important to maintain flexibility for adaptation to consumer behavior and market changes, in addition to the sudden opportunities that may arise, such as, the CBSE circular for schools[2] that benefitted YoScholar's business.

Using Social Media

Social media emerged about two decades ago and have left startup founders incapable to understand them fully. This statement is based on input from people across the board. Hence, they often land up hiring the wrong people and working with the wrong agencies for social media engagements. It is due to this reason that this revolutionary marketing tool is still not being integrated well by companies in the early stages of developing a total marketing tool.

The 20 odd companies I worked with gave me an impression that they considered social media to be a marketing tool by default rather than carrying out proper research and planning to determine which marketing channels are most relevant to their specific needs. So, counseling them to map their requirements and marketing strategies to the available marketing communication tools became a very important part of my advisory. In our engagements thereafter, we started to clearly demarcate demographic groups, brand message, unique selling proposition (USP), if any, and other factors that can differentiate the companies from competition.

One of the very impactful VPs I have worked with (and we continue to collaborate) is Apurva Chamaria. His thoughts on the

---

[2] CBSE had released a circular to check on the commercial activities on school campuses. The notice said that the institutions under their mandate will not undertake activities of sales and purchase of school supplies on campus.

role of digital marketing for startups are bang on. According to him, with both competitors and potential customers constantly online, an important way to stay ahead is by getting the timing of digital marketing right. A big part of marketing strategy is digital. Any business can compete with any competitor, regardless of size, with a solid digital marketing strategy.

As a starting point, here are some research activities to get you started with your small business digital marketing plan:

- *Customer profiles:* Which types of customers visit your website and then convert to a lead or sale? How does this differ compared to other traditional channels? It is advised that businesses of all sizes should have target personalities or "pen portraits" of at least two to three customer types.

- *Customer search behavior research:* Determine how your prospects search for a solution to satisfy their needs— understanding the volume and type of customer intent is vital when you are looking to grab more share of search as people search for your products or services.

- *Competitor research:* You can run a profitable website without considering competitors, but a review as part of the planning will definitely give ideas and is essential to spot opportunities and weaknesses as part of the SWOT analysis.

- *Influencer, partner, and intermediary research:* What type of people and other websites influence your audience as they look for your product and service? This angle is often neglected, but partnerships and certain types of influencers can be a great source of low-cost, good-quality traffic.

- *Current business effectiveness:* Mine your sales data, since every number has a story. Dissect each element of the data generated in terms of preferences, reach, preferred channel of engagement, and reasons to buy. Well-analyzed data always provide deeper insights to the thoughts of a consumer.

Customers and businesses alike are almost always online, and digital marketing strategy comes in handy to reach them and observe their behavior where they spend most of their time. A series of actions helps to achieve the desired goal(s) using online marketing. Several low-cost digital marketing strategies for the startups are listed here.

- *Search marketing:* Search engine optimization (SEO) is the key to increasing website traffic. The startups must know the keywords that rank among the top three organic results. In case it is an e-commerce website, it will require paid search marketing activities to display the products to the website visitors.

- *Marketing funnel creation:* The technique of conversion rate optimization (CRO) should be used for understanding why visitors are not "converting" into customers, and then improving the messaging or value proposition to increase this rate of conversion, which can be done by understanding the visitors' requirements and reservations. The most successful businesses have an effective marketing funnel in place. This includes mapping out a typical customer's journey from a complete stranger to a lead, and then putting certain strategies in place that will encourage them to move through this funnel.

- *Landing page optimization:* The landing page of any startup is one of the crucial factors in generating leads for its products and then ultimately making business by selling those products. The landing page must be good enough to compel visitors to get converted into customers.

- *Internal pages optimization:* There are free and cheap solutions available for optimizing the internal pages for conversion. Free plug-ins can be used for capturing emails and then leveraging affordable services such as MailChimp for drip campaigns. Free tools such as Google Analytics can be used to monitor visitors' paths to the website and find opportunities to create a more user-friendly experience once they are on it. Forms on websites can be optimized to build a stronger inbound lead funnel. Cheap and reliable cart services are available to sell products directly through the company website.

- *Content marketing:* Content marketing, which can be done by engaging in industry research and formulating USPs, is one of the most overlooked investments in launching a startup. Visually stimulating content with appealing imagery and minimal words score a lot when it comes to websites. However, that cannot diminish the power of captivating words, and they are as good as pictures. One of the most important steps to an effective content marketing strategy is content promotion. Amplify it as much as possible. Leverage social media profiles, email industry experts, reach out to LinkedIn groups or industry forums, and contribute to other popular sites that your target customers might visit.

- *Email marketing:* Email marketing is now becoming one of the best digital marketing weapons which will help a startup not only promote its brand but also generate leads to make business for the brand.

- *Social media marketing:* Social media are one of the most cost-effective ways to market startups. In addition to providing a platform for growing the brand, they offer an easy medium for promotion and customer service opportunities. They are a way to build the brand voice, which can be done at a frequent and consistent pace. They can be used to find and share customer-related information. Many social media platforms and search engines feature paid advertisements, which any startup can easily afford, as most of these paid ads start with a minimum budget of $10. You can also further increase the budget according to your requirement to gain a much better reach among the target audience. There are a number of different social opportunities that one can invest in, all of which have merit depending on the industry and the product's USP. Facebook is steadily becoming a pay-to-play platform, and, to see any engagement, one can invest in Facebook posts promotion. While Twitter still provides a good amount of organic engagement, the microblogging platform also has paid solutions for businesses, including sponsored tweets. Sponsored tweets can lead to higher engagement, creating followers. LinkedIn has a number of extremely valuable paid features, including a Sales Navigator that makes finding leads and contacts seamless. One of the biggest benefits of social media for business is using it to increase website traffic. Not only does social media help direct people to a website, but the more social media shares received, the higher the search ranking will be.

- *Multichannel strategy:* A digital marketing strategy should always be multichannel in nature. It helps cover every possible segment of your target audience. For example, blogs help generate interest and provide opinions/reviews for potential customers, thus helping them choose between alternatives. YouTube podcasts help customers by informing them about the products.

Running a startup on a shoestring budget is quite hard. By keeping the marketing costs down while capitalizing successfully on digital opportunities, one will be able to improve brand visibility without employing a large budget.

Finally, I had quite a simple and really relevant message for all the companies I engaged with: *If they can provide a consistent brand and campaign message, which is tuned to audience requirements, there is an effective integrated campaign.* Simulanis initially started promotions using only print promotional material, but they quickly moved to showcasing their services during events and speaking in seminars. While delivering the message, the founders had to be clear that the print material being left for the audience resonates with what has been spoken. They have some ground to cover in terms of the UI/UX of their social and physical presence. However, Raman, the founder of Simulanis, uses Twitter very effectively. The moment he delivers a talk, the highlights are tweeted before he forgets them. This ensures that the core message is delivered, resonating across all customer touch points.

Taking to the World

Once the companies in my portfolio got their branding strategy right in terms of the name, logo, effective display, and a universally acceptable domain name, it was time to announce their arrival. The websites of these companies became a gateway to the consumer universe by ensuring that the website visitors leave their registered email ids, and potentially become early adopters, and, later, assessors of the app to be launched in due course of time. Based on these learning experiences, ClassBoat, Ahhaa, AmbitionUp, and Simulanis redid their websites in order to reflect their world-class approach and strong solutions.

There were many digital marketing strategies adopted by the companies to ensure that website visitors also shared their visits with their own networks. This ultimately helped to capture an invaluable customer database, which would help in building up a repository of contact details of people who may be interested in the offerings—the potential users.

All the aforementioned measures to reach out to the virtual world laid the foundation for creating a high-impact service (now known as ClassBoat, addressing 6,000–8,000 users per month @ ₹4 lakhs per month revenue) that would change the way consumers use digital media to discover their passion and find the right sources to help them learn new things. This ClassBoat platform helped consumers create a career development roadmap in a short span of time. Process efficiency and leveraging first-mover advantage became the pillars of their success.

Speed or Precision?

For many startups, it is very difficult to choose between chasing precision and executing with speed—the portfolios I worked with were no different—and I would say, "precision always". A lot of startups think that they already know what kind of e-service and/or mobile app will be acceptable to people. This makes them work on the concept, design, and development of a complicated and feature-rich proposition, which they feel is complete and comprehensive. Once the product/service is perceptually ready, it is launched, marketing burn rate hits the roof, the media is all over the place; yet, a very few people actually buy it, and startups begin to jitter. I have experienced this first hand when I advised TinyTapps. The company had tested their product on 300 tablets and were ready to go to market. However, they faced the usual challenges of telecom product performance and had to deal with the nuances of after-sales support for mobile tablets. TinyTapps is not a telecom product management company, its core is pre-school content. However, they got dragged into selling and servicing hardware.

Traditionally, startups believe that the e-service/app must be made quickly (choosing speed over precision), frugally, and with energy and vision for the future. It is felt that with speedy implementation, the uncertainty can be minimized, followed up by rigorous focus on evolving, developing, and testing the product, so that the revisions keep on making sense to the target audience. It may be true that speed may be able to invoke the best judgment in a critical situation and leads to smart work more than hard work. The moment a prototype/beta/minimum viable product reaches the hands of the user, a very precious output called *feedback* becomes available. For example, user feedback made Edvantics go back to the drawing board while Vidya Robotics realized that it was possible to create a world-class product, but they were still a bit far from it. All-important feedback is relevant until the time the startup has a way to measure, analyze, and take corrective/preventive action to ensure that the product is making sense and is viable for the end user.

The speed versus precision decision often comes up when the web interface has to transition to a mobile app.

In the End

Integrated marketing is a mindset that comes with great difficulty to tech startup founders; it is a tool that can make or break brands. Startups that focus on IMC strategies early on get a kick start, which ensures that the customer experiences a consistent brand interaction across the board.

An integrated approach also opens up new channels of business communication which might not have been thought about earlier—referrals, people as brand ambassadors, to name a few. In a world that people are exploring through their smartphones and tablets, it is important to remember that traditional marketing still holds good, as is testified by Simulanis, YoScholar, and Ahhaa. However, in the digital landscape, startups have the chance to attract a captive audience by using interactive gamification and simple content feed. One must still know that promoting a website is different from promoting an app, and each should have its own differentiated strategy. *The core theme must be to integrate digital presence into a more holistic integrated campaign management with assessable outcomes.*

APPENDIX: Integrated Marketing Communication (IMC) Plan

Audience Analysis

Objective

Awareness

Database

Acquisition

Stimulate sales

Transaction

Retention

Remove Myths

What does your audience currently know about you?

What medium do they access most often?

Are you trying to influence a negative attitude the audience has toward you or the space you operate in?

Competitor Campaigns

Include an analysis of your competitors (present and anticipatory)

Present competition:

Anticipatory competition:

Communication objectives:

Target audiences:

Creative concepts and messages:

Media selection:

Promotional tactics:

Communication Strategy

Campaign impact and duration

Is the overall marketing strategy to skim or penetrate the market rapidly?

How long will the campaign last and what is the timing of each element?

Creative Strategy

Develop an overall theme, appeal, and message concept.

Do you have an integrated brand guideline and personality communication strategy?

Do you have a standard corporate template for

Presentations ▢

Leaflets ▢

Brochures ▢

Online mailers ▢

Banners ▢

Key Considerations (for information of companies)

Ensure that brand personality is embedded in all media.

There should be no isolated promotional items; avoid random, ill redirected, or ill-timed collaterals.

All media should be linked, each one dependent on another.

Think existing touch points—where existing clients/customers already interact with your brand, marketing communications, and customer facing points, such as employees.

Keep a consistent "look and feel" across all design elements.

Promotional Strategy and Budgets (Strike Out the Elements that Are Not Relevant)

What's your action plan and budget for the next six months on the following?

Element	Traditional Media	Technology	Budget	Remarks
Advertising (ATL and BTL)[a] Objectives	Print TV Brochures Leaflets OOH[b] Radio B2B sales pitch	YouTube Google Facebook MySpace Instagram LinkedIn		
PR and Publicity Objectives	Authored articles Press releases Media events (announcements) Corporate events Sponsorships Press calls Publicity stunts	Online articles and blogs Bloggers' interviews Sponsorships		
Direct Marketing Objectives	Target List • Door to Door • Creative mailers through post • Social gatherings	Target List Email campaigns SMS campaigns Viral campaigns		
Sales Promotions Objectives	• Free sampling • Competitions • Onsite activation with free elements (merchandize) • Loss leading (buying the customer)	• Online free access (limited period) • Online competitions • Online discount codes		

Notes: [a]ATL: Above-the-line advertising. This includes television, print, and radio advertising done in broadcast mode. It is not customized and is impersonal. BTL: Below-the-line advertising, leveraging posters, brochures, leaflets, flyers, and tent cards. BTL is customized specifically to the target audience and can be changed more regularly.

[b]OOH: Out-of-home advertising including billboards, hoardings, vehicle advertising, and bus shelters as medium of marketing communication.

Implementation Timeline (Box the Element Relevant to Each Month)

Month	Advertising	PR and Publicity	Direct Marketing	Sales Promotions	Budget
April					
May					
June					
July					
August					
Sept					

CHAPTER 4

Business on a Shoestring

Shoestring refers to a small or inadequate budget, and startup owners are well versed with this term. Most startup founders work with shoestring budgets, as they do not have the luxury of getting friends and family to invest or external investors who are enthused enough at the first mention of the minimum viable product (MVP). Funding a startup from your own pocket is an enormous challenge, and the first few months call for austere measures. And austerity is a virtue that is unrelated to age, wisdom, and maturity. Many startup founders have taken the *bootstrapping route*—funding a business out of one's own money; and being austere is not optional for them but is the only way. First-time startup owners find it difficult to get funding for their projects, and they may decide to fund them themselves for a while until they are ready to approach investors.

Only few startups, such as Abroad Shiksha, with the founders' family business to fall back on and money ready to be invested, can afford to have luxurious offices to begin with. However, for every such case, there are several others not as comfortably placed. Bootstrapping is often much more difficult than what it may seem initially. The founders of ClassBoat ran their office out of one of their homes for two years in order to be cost efficient, until some investor could pour money into the startup. Do you really need first-hand furniture, brand new IT infrastructure, and a posh office? All of this can be managed through shared resources and second-hand equipment. It is wise to save every penny that can be used to procure critical resources needed for developing the core product.

When the cofounders of ReadRush created their startup, they used personal funds for a while, but soon realized that the well was drying up fast. They had to immediately seek external investors, which led to a slower pace of growth. However, they remained steadfast and were able to tide over the crisis. Even for ClassBoat, it took 12 months to ramp up their revenue from ₹30,000 to ₹400,000 per month. They soon generated traction, and, after that, it took only 8–12 weeks for external investors to express interest. Until then, ClassBoat survived on bootstrapping with money from friends and family. If entrepreneurs play their cards right, they can achieve significant growth and a payoff that's well worth the wait.

Bootstrapping is a lesson in patience, adaptability, resilience, and flexibility. It is worth all the trouble and ultimately helps bring a company success. There are some common bootstrapping elements that make all the difference to startups. I have noted the key elements—discussed in the following sections—time and again while working with different startups.

Look for Complementary Skills in the Core Team

ClassBoat, YoScholar, Abroad Shiksha, and KidsTriangle made a strategic deep dive into their social networks to find people with complementary skills. While bootstrapping, the majority of work has to be done internally, so it is important for cofounders and core team members to complement each other's skills as much as possible. The core team members hired initially by these companies had skills that ensured the companies got a good shot at being able to do everything in-house, which kept the expenses very low. They did not outsource any job required for the business. One important lesson I learnt while interacting with these passionate founders was that the clarity they had on what all can be done in-house. When bootstrapping, hiring for a job you can do yourself is an expense that must be avoided. The case study provided later in this chapter will present real-life examples.

Ensure Faster Cash Flow

A great example of a successful bootstrapping strategy was demonstrated by the founder of Simulanis, Raman. He used his personal resources to build the company; he converted his home basement into a state-of-the art office. However, the bigger challenge was to ensure undivided focus in order to reduce time to revenue. He made it evident that the faster you generate revenue the more successful will be the ways to bootstrap.[1] The most successful bootstrapped companies have the common feature of being able to generate cash at the earliest. One must not let the

---

[1] While Raman had his mind set on creating a great VR platform, he started off with a consulting assignment and launching SARAL books with AR. These streams started giving the company quick revenue and reduced the time to market.

company gasp for funds even before the customer starts to pay for their product/service.

Austerity at All Levels

Is show-off important to create a perception about a company? If your answer is yes, then think again. The most bootstrapped companies have not believed in this. It is important to ensure that cost-optimized options are chosen. Initially it is important to pick office spaces that are more functionally viable rather than swanky. The founders I worked with preferred a place closer to home that did not have a state-of-the-art setup but offered a table and chair, Wi-Fi, and a coffee-vending machine. It ensures they burn less fuel to travel to and from home, and the money that is saved comes in handy to pay for overheads. They would get visiting cards published from online media, which are cost-optimized. When hiring people, they would prefer giving them refurbished computers rather than picking new ones.

It is also essential to manage company expenses and personal expenses separately. Many founders make the mistake of using the same bank account for personal and company-related expenses. It is advisable to use expense management tools to be able to ascertain the difference between a must-have versus a good-to-have asset, while keeping a hawk's-eye on the expenses. We have seen company founders with years of erstwhile high-profile jobs travelling in overnight buses when they launched their own startups.

Being prudent and frugal with no compromise on the effective output is an art and needs to be mastered well. Small savings go a long way to make a big contribution. It is a culture to be imbibed early in the startup's life cycle.

Along with bootstrapping comes a natural sacrifice by founders—their salary. So suddenly, for professionals previously enjoying six-figure salaries, there were no monthly funds to spare for a posh lifestyle. Still they scraped through at every step, spending only on what was absolutely essential. TrisLabs, established by a team of founders from Birla Institute of Technology and Science (BITS) Pilani, hounded us until the time we arranged to get two free co-working seats in Bangalore for them (courtesy Echidna). The founder of MuseIn, an IIM Kozhikode and IIT Madras alumnus, decided to shift base with family from Hyderabad to Bangalore in order to save on rent and related out-of-pocket expenses. Suddenly, these companies had more money in hand to spend on essential resources and meetings rather than burn on cost of living.

Unlearning and Learning

Another critical aspect of bootstrapping is *unlearning and learning*. Many seasoned professionals who become startup founders get fixated in their existing skill sets and ways of working. Jay, the founder of ClassBoat, was very candid about being a specialist in marketing and strategy but not in sales. However, the moment he embraced the art of selling, the husband–wife duo took the company from a revenue of ₹30,000 per month to ₹600,000 per month. Just by acquiring the skill of sales engagement, the founders achieved two things: (a) saved the salary of salespeople and (b) got a good grip on the sales funnel and strategic relationships. The bottom line is that, as a founder, if one does not know how to do something, there is always time to learn it. You may be very surprised by your inherent and unexplored abilities.

Exploring All Options

Every company starts with creating their digital presence first, which usually starts with the company website. Now, people like me, who have managed corporations, know that the way to go about a website is to get a developer on the job. This comes at a cost, and the quality of the work may not be assured. I got personal advice from someone to explore readymade templates in case only an infographic website was needed. And that worked for me, as I got my personal website [www.meetrishi.com] created by a coder. The flow and texture of the website was already in the template; all it needed was good content.

Along with web domain registration, another application of bootstrapping is in the area of legality and compliances. Many company founders use online incorporation services, but end up with complications that cost more in the long run. Also, online incorporation services are for founders who know about legality and compliances better than laymen. EDUGILD works with reputed legal firms to provide compliance and due-diligence services for various startups. There is a specific example of a company called Ahhaa.com, which changed its incorporation from New York to India. They were in the early stages of their startup and could not afford legal fees. So, our partner legal company came out with a viable solution where the fee was broken into payments over the span of a year—a win-win situation for both parties, effectively spreading out the risk thin during the bootstrapping phase.

Knowing When to Change Tack

How long to continue to bootstrap depends on the ability to realign and reject. Every startup has one goal—to get as much traction as possible to raise customer confidence and, in turn, attract investors purely based on performance. The need to generate revenues brings about such tricky and uncertain situations at times that it feels as though everything that has been done until now is a waste. Such randomly encountered tricky opportunities may tempt the founders to change/modify the operational model and even tweak the product offering. This becomes very depressing, especially when hard-earned money has already been put into the present working model. Bootstrapping is useful only if the company's offering satisfies the consumers being targeted.

We encountered a first-hand experience related to this with ClassBoat. After almost a year, ClassBoat was plateauing at a revenue of ₹30,000–50,000 per month with a monthly burn rate of ₹350,000. There came a time when survival without external funding was looking impossible. There had to be an end to the bootstrapping phase. So, one fine day, the founders sat with their strategic advisors. Well-meaning advisors and well-wishers will always provide ruthless, matter-of-fact feedback rather than sugarcoat the message. So, in this meeting, ClassBoat was clearly told that they are going away from the consumer's pulse and will steadily continue to lose the ground won so far. While the founders had a bewildered look, the advisors were cold and stoic. Now, slowly and steadily, the use cases, consumer behavior, and target segment characteristics got defined, and ClassBoat was advised to completely transform their current model. The founders, Jay and Renu, left the room with confusion visible through their body language, and then they went back to the drawing board. Around 72 hours later, they came out with a cost analysis—what it would cost to change tack. The interesting part was that no cost escalation was expected in this situation, but it would need Jay to be on the road as a salesman as much as Renu and other salespeople in the team.

The company tasted success early with this change and realized that course providers who have the capacity to pay, that is, those who offer courses with fees of more than ₹25,000, will be able to generate revenue for ClassBoat. Keeping the costs in check, and identifying 10 prospects that could afford ClassBoat services, the company cracked half of them in the first month and the revenue jumped to ₹200,000 in that month. This was a six-fold rise in month-on-month revenue. However, was this revenue level sustainable? The entire credit goes to the founders for ensuring the sustainability of this level of revenue, while bootstrapping at the core. While maintaining austerity, they went from pillar to post (in fact, lost a few resources but doubled up in those roles themselves), and demonstrated an average revenue of ₹350,000 per month over the next three months. This gave confidence to the ecosystem that the revenue jump was not just a blip but was the effect of realigning at the right time. Finally, in the subsequent months, the company touched a revenue of ₹500,000–700,000 per month. With this, they broke even, gained immense self-confidence, and were now working on a seven-city expansion and diversification strategy. This is what happens when opportunities are evaluated well, seized at the right time, and aligned to long-term company goals. One must also be able to reject any opportunities that could be a big distraction from their set goals.

Mullins' seven domains model[2] offers very good lessons in bootstrapping—connectedness up, down, and across the value chain is all about not taking a "no" for an answer. Bootstrapping

---

[2] John Mullins, "What to Teach Before Your Business Plan Course," PowerPoint Presentation, accessed February 10, 2018, https://web. stanford.edu/group/ree/archives/archive11/la/presentations/Mullins% 20-%20Tulsa%20Turkey%20Won't%20Fly%20Sept%202011.pdf

strategies require startups to critically evaluate their people network connections and their importance to the success of the business. It is a fact that vendors and suppliers do not like to work with early-stage companies, for example, manufacturers turn a blind eye to small requirements such as 100 t-shirts as branding merchandise. Such showstopper requirements need to be managed more on personal terms rather than on business lines. A bootstrapping company needs high credit time, low product-manufacturing cost, and no limits of minimum order quantities, and such favors can only be extended by a friend or family in the supply chain. A bootstrapper must ensure that they jot down the names of all the people among their relations who can be suppliers, sales partners, or customers, who will make a leap of faith with the startup. Our portfolio companies, TinyTapps and YoScholar, became customer acquisition partners for each other, since both of them developed mutual confidence when they engaged with EDUGILD. This initiative helped obtain the resources needed to get the companies going without bankrupting the founders. In order to be true bootstrappers, we realized that the founders have to persevere until the answers to all their problems are found.

SPOTLIGHT: Ekin Knowledge—edWhizz by Ekin

Ekin Knowledge is an innovative edtech company in the space of personalized learning. edWhizz by Ekin Knowledge is a cloud-based, mobile-first personalized learning platform that enables teachers to deliver differentiated instructions and personalized assessments based on student needs. edWhizz enhances deeper learning and drives student success with a personalized learning experience based on individual needs in the classroom.

The Founders

Preetham's partner Seralathan Devaraju is a successful entrepreneur running a multimillion dollar IT services business. Preetham has over 20 years of experience, cutting across technology, consulting, business analysis, and extensive international exposure, in various domains such as e-commerce, telecom, and healthcare. So, they both had tech and consulting backgrounds, which were complementary skills for the venture they wanted to start.

The Ekin Genesis

In 2014, when they started, there were hardly any major edtech investments happening. This was primarily because of the failure to sustain growth of some big names in India's edtech scenario, and this had a massive adverse impact on investor confidence in edtech ventures. Having been part of the IT service industry from the .com days, the founders of Ekin were well aware of the pitfalls of attempting product development, especially in the education domain, which has a very small appetite for risk-taking and change.

Owing to their experience, the founders realized that between them they had the skills to execute most of the critical aspects of product development. While Seran took control of the technical aspects of product development, Preetham acquired the requisite domain knowledge to define the roadmap and vision for the product. In the early stages, they made the grave mistake of burning too much of money by hiring tech and other operational staff in the hope that once they get past the MVP phase, they would be able to secure funding for GTM and growth. They quickly realized that depending on investors to fund the early stages without revenues in place would be a pipe dream, and started working toward building a low-burn model, through which they could conserve cash for the long run.

Choosing Implementation Partners Well

By the end of the first year, Ekin had laid-off most of the full-time employees and started working with freelance resources, maintaining a lean team and controlling the core aspects of product development, such as, design, architecture, product roadmap, and user experience. Most of the tech work was outsourced to freelance developers. This was still a challenge, as the top-end freelance resources were always working for large companies, and getting their time was difficult; so, they started working on weekends with these freelance resources. It took longer than usual to develop the product, but this way they ensured that they worked on a tight budget. As the product became more complex, it was becoming difficult to work with freelancers. This is when Ekin decided to engage a company so that they could be sure that the quality does not suffer. This is where EDUGILD and my contribution came into the picture, as we scouted for the right tech development partner for Ekin. Even with a partner product development company, Ekin got into a fixed bid arrangement, since getting into a typical time and material contract would not allow them the freedom to work within their budgets. It is imperative to be selective with the partners and consultants one spends time with.

Avoiding Distractions During the Early Stages

The market is flooded with companies that provide consulting services for startups on various aspects such as business planning, financial planning, funding, and networking, but they will not be able to help the founders with execution, customer acquisition, or funding unless the founders build a value proposition for the product. The onus is on the founder to find a way to sustain the startup until the revenue stage is reached. Time is the most precious commodity when you want to convert your idea into a tangible product.

Bootstrapping to Success

"When one is building a ship, one does not begin with gathering timber and cutting planks, but rather by arousing in people the yearning for experiencing the great wide sea." Delays, failures, realignments, and challenges are an intrinsic part of a startup's journey, but what makes a true entrepreneur is the ability to overcome these obstacles and keep the ship sailing through rough seas to reach the destination.

The startup world is completely sold out to the ethos of bootstrapping, and Indian or Silicon Valley startups are no exceptions. How exactly did a married couple with no aggregation-based business expertise create ClassBoat and get to ₹500,000–600,000 per month of revenue? How did the Ekin founders let go of their comfort zones and bootstrap to success?

There is also a lesson to be learnt from the TinyTapps experience of bootstrapping. Altaf, the company founder, is a go-getter. Before we came to know each other, the company had already created a content delivery strategy through mobile tablets. During the opportunity assessment phase, TinyTapps were advised to avoid the inventory trap, especially since they were bootstrapped. However, since the team had already progressed in that strategic direction, not much could have been done. However, it became clear early enough that effectively managing orders in the early days will be a huge challenge, along with incurring the cost to repair/replace/service product outages. Managing supply and demand became a challenge, as inventory kept dragging ahead and the liquidation strategy was yet to kick in. Fortunately, the founders simultaneously established a cloud- and USB-based service delivery model, which eliminated the need for customized mobile tablets.

Finally, the general guideline that has worked well in terms of funding is to avoid early venture capital (VC) calls. Startups usually lack the ability to deal with VC calls effectively during their early days. The companies I work with sometimes get very excited when they get calls from investment analysts of VC firms, and I keep telling them that the analysts are simply doing their job—venture hunting as many prospects as possible. However, it is in no way an ultimate validation of the efforts of the startups. So, the smart founders kept diplomatic relationships with early callers from VCs, but promised to get back only when the proposition is solid. In return, the startups earned a lot of respect and regular recall from the investing community.

So, while soliciting early funding may seem tempting, it may not be the right redemption of success. Bootstrapping has several advantages and should be enjoyed as long as possible. First, it helps the company founders stay cautious and alert, and discover unknown talents and skills in themselves. Second, it helps them remained closely involved in the day-to-day affairs, which matters while hiring talent.

Bootstrapping techniques helped these startups fast-track their way to success. As things began to get tough for some, they went on an austerity overdrive or changed tack rather than sulk and look for sympathy. We all agree that bootstrapping is hard, but the forces that work in its favor bring out zeal, creativity, innovative intelligence, and novel solutions to the fore.

Make Me, Break Me, Remake Me

The Leaner the Meaner

Of the approximately 500 startup founders I have spoken to in the last two years, several have dreamt of coming up with a tech solution that will change the world. However, did they seriously contemplate about what they thought people needed? Too many entrepreneurs launch into designing and developing a technical product that no one is willing to spend on. Thus, they end up already having pumped-in in excess of $200,000 into a technology solution with no way to amortize it.

Here is what happens at the so-called lean startups (which has become a buzzword): They carry out research on a small sample, and most of the times claim to be creating a solution to a problem they have faced personally; but then, who is going to pay for solutions to someone else's personal problem statements? Also, what gets missed in such ventures is the amount of time that is needed to be spent convincing the prospective adopters of the application/service/product.

At MIT's EDUGILD, India's first edtech startup accelerator, I was lucky enough to get to work not just with mature founders but also with tech partners such as DoodleBlue, who actually created the technology for two of our companies. Over a period of time, we interacted with Josh Software Private Ltd and Hyphenos Software Labs Private Ltd in Pune, and found amazing people who create top-class technology with a pragmatic approach. Gautam Naidu of Talentica in Pune really influenced our view about tech and product evolution in companies. He is an amazing person and has been a part of our startups assessment committee ever since; he has never missed any onboarding program at EDUGILD. Talentica is a clear evidence of how a strong tech partner can change a company's stakes. Technology evolution is a short-span activity, and the cost of replication is going down. Hence, it is important to build tech that is sustainable, scalable, and reasonable.

Based on discussions with the various advisors and experts we approached for understanding the technology needs of startups, there were a few common learnings primarily related to the choice of technology, which impacts cost, scalability, and launch schedules of the startups' propositions. For example, while SkillSoniq was clearly looking to get their tech platform developed on RoR (Ruby on Rails), MuseIn wanted to have their solution hosted on Python, and the Edvantics team had a knack for tech, being ex-Intel and ex-Microsoft, but with the understanding that it was important for the co-founders to be on the same page. Now these technical names are Greek to many, including me. However, nailing the right tech stack, as they say, is the key to a sound start.

So let us list the questions that each company must answer faithfully and with careful thought.

1. If you already have a tech team, what is their background?

Do the tech team have worthwhile experience of building what you are proposing to build or only some but not a great deal? (Note that coming from great engineering colleges alone does not help here.) It is perfectly fine not to have a decent enough tech team; clarity about how and when you are going to build one is good enough. If you instead plan to "outsource" completely at least two challenges you have thought about in implementing this strategy. While I was myself on the outsourcing side of the table, I now know that the reality out there is rather bleak, so a more than basic understanding of the challenges involved is absolutely necessary.

2. What does your tech stack look like?

What is your best understanding of the technologies you are planning to use? (Note that terms such as deep learning/ML/NLP/NoSQL sound very sophisticated but are quite "high level.") It is okay not to have this clarity at the start, but it would be of immense help if you can start thinking along the following lines: "We plan to build our application as REST API developed in Django REST framework (or RoR REST framework) and the client side will be written in React/React Native as appropriate. We are planning to use a mix of NoSQL and SQL databases with some caching layer."

For this question, it is okay to err on the side of communicating more rather than communicating less.

3. What was the rationale behind choosing this tech stack?

To this question, an answer such as "our current tech team was most comfortable with it" is perfectly fine. Not all tech platforms need to have sophisticated and high-cost mobile apps for all platforms, a web app, a backend, and a database. It all depends upon the stage the company is in (MVP, beta, early revenue, or steady revenue).

4. What traffic did you plan this for?

Is this an infographic-only solution or a transactional solution? Designing for a billion page views is a great thought, but one needs to get more realistic about the practicality of it. So something along these lines is appropriate: We foresee these many users in the first X months and this is how they will use the system, so this is a rough estimate of the traffic we plan to serve. It is prudent to think about how much monitoring and analyzing the solution will need as compared to just making a high-capacity platform.

5. What will your deployment strategy be?

The tech stack has to and must align to the business strategy. The consumers are not interested in knowing the technological platform being used: They pay for what the technology delivers. So, redundancy, business continuity, and load balancing are critical aspects. For example, how long do you think that the following strategy will be viable/economical: being completely on a cloud platform such as AWS/Google Cloud/Azure or running on a virtual private server (VPS), a virtual machine sold as a service by an Internet hosting service, and doing everything yourself? Again, it is okay not to have full answers to these questions, but one must generally keep in mind the next steps. The technical complexity must be balanced against the customer impact, cost, and overall business needs. These factors will ultimately decide the strategy that will work the best for you.

6. What are your engineering practices?

Do your developers extensively use version control, continuous deployment, and unit testing? If the answers to these questions are "yes," then you have a strong case.

7. What was the hardest technical problem your tech team has solved?

The problem described does not have to be one faced in the current company. This is a trick question to evaluate the thought process and problem-solving acumen of the tech person/team.

Let me now take the example of Edvantics to illustrate how the tech/MVP should be associated with the business strategy and the vision of the founders.

Sharat and Sirisha first met on a Google hangouts call in Spring 2014. The call was scheduled as a "get to know each other" virtual catch-up for the Indian School of Business (ISB) admits based out of the USA. After more than 12 years in the USA, both moved back to India in Summer 2014 with their respective families to pursue their MBA programs at ISB. Sirisha had moved to the USA in 2001 after her Bachelor of Engineering course to pursue her masters course at Santa Clara University. After graduating, she worked briefly at Cypress Semiconductors and then joined Intel. She had been with Intel for 11 years before she moved back to India for her MBA. Sharat had moved to the USA in 2002 to pursue a masters in information systems course from Texas A&M International University. He then worked as a business intelligence and data analytics consultant for a boutique data analytics-consulting firm called iTech US Inc. for seven years. He then went independent as a consultant with IBM Information Management practice, working on engagements in data and predictive analytics for four years before moving back to India.

The time spent at ISB helped both of them understand the Indian context better for businesses and startups. They ran into each other quite often at entrepreneurship-related events and naturally started exchanging thoughts and ideas. Coincidentally, they both landed offers at Microsoft in Hyderabad as senior project managers. *Entrepreneurship is an itch that needs to be scratched.* Microsoft is a great organization to work for, especially in the era of Satya Nadella as its CEO, when all the employees' spirits were soaring high. However, both Sirisha and Sharat continued to discuss multiple ideas, most of which happened to be around kids, parenting, and education. Being parents themselves and having a strong inclination toward coaching younger minds, edtech was more a chance than a choice.

In their research, they realized that academics-related aspirations, opportunities, and market offerings are deeply inter-connected but rarely integrated to derive value for all stakeholders across the academic life cycle. With their backgrounds in data insights projects and analytics consulting, they decided to exploit the power of data insights and machine learning to create value for both students and institutes. As part of their research and keeping in mind their long-term strategy, they partnered with their local state government's skill and knowledge division (TASK—Telangana Academy for Skill and Knowledge—has a tie up with around 550+ institutes) to offer free career counseling at colleges in their city. In exchange, they got their feet in the door to talk to principals, management boards of educational institutes, and students to understand the ground reality. These engagements helped them to understand the key pain points of end users as well as get clarity on the market needs. The next couple of months were spent in designing the offering they had in mind, and an MVP was carved out of a grand vision.

A high-level operational cost assessment was done to get an idea of what it would take to execute this MVP and the grand vision. Both Sirisha and Sharat were confident that they could bootstrap the effort and execute it with lean operations and personal funds. Both their spouses also encouraged them to pursue their passion full time. Sharat left Microsoft to co-found Edvantics and soon Sirisha followed. The idea was to spend ₹2 millions of their savings on the development of their MVP and thereafter gain some traction before reaching out to angel investors—a critical move since bootstrapping had to be in their DNA rather than a choice. They started by creating wireframes for the MVP and then hired a freelance graphic designer to create the logo, website, and product mock-ups.

They then applied for Microsoft's BizSpark program to get the infrastructure taken care of, and luckily got accepted. Through friends and ISB contacts, they shortlisted two services companies that could develop their product and finalized one of them for the development of their minimum viable version. Their early and continuous engagement with TASK helped them identify opportunities for product features that were the need of the hour for many academic institutes. Further, this also helped onboard a few Tier 1 institutes to pilot the MV version. Once convinced of their ability to gain some traction, they started to explore fund raising, with the realization that they will need more resources to go to market.

After a few initial discussions with some angel investors and a few failed attempts at incubators, they soon realized that fundraising is a distractor rather than an enabler. They sat down to relook at what would the operations cost for a year from that point, and realized that with an additional $150,000, they could put together a small team and execute the work until they started generating revenues. Being very conscious about operating lean, both founders spent every dime on product development as much as possible and negotiated Series A tied contracts with legal counsel, digital marketing advisors, and accounting firms.

For every need, they leveraged free or startup-friendly offerings. Fortunately for them, some friends and family members came together and the initial capital was raised on convertible notes terms. After working at the ISB campus for the first couple of months, they took up a co-working space in Hyderabad and started putting together a team. Out of the blue, I discovered them while venture-hunting as the CEO of EDUGILD, and we asked them to make their pitch. As EDUGILD is an edtech-focused accelerator in India, both Sirisha and Sharat believed that it will be highly beneficial for their growth. After a few rounds of discussions and personal meetings, EDUGILD offered to onboard Edvantics for their fourth batch of the program in September 2017. Now, ever since EDUGILD came along, their venture is on a treadmill of acceleration.

Now to illustrate answers to the tech questions raised earlier, Exhibit 5.1 lists down the real-life responses given by Edvantics.[1]

---

[1] Based on a report generated using the EDUGILD Technology Diagnostic Assessment Report Tool.

EXHIBIT 5.1   Edvantics Product and Technology Journey

If you already have a tech team, what is their background?

Development till date has been outsourced. However, we have been very active in the last two months to build an in-house tech team. We have recently hired a UI developer who has expertise in Angular JS. We are in the process of interviewing for senior product architect and back-end and front-end developer roles as part of the first phase of our hiring. For Phase 2 of the hiring, we plan to bring data engineers onboard to help develop the recommendation engine for the application.

We currently have a senior architect from Microsoft advising us on a weekly/biweekly basis on our architecture and product development strategies.

What does your tech stack look like?

Our application is built on PHP and MySQL. No framework has been used till date. However, as per a detailed analysis of all the features we plan to integrate on our platform, we plan to continue using PHP for the back end, MySQL for database management, and Angular JS for the front end.

Another key area for us is building a recommendation engine. Based on our research and for our requirements, the optimal choice seems to be Python or Scala. However, we are hoping for our data science resources to be able to assess the application requirements and help us decide accordingly.

What was the rationale behind choosing this tech stack?

Our tech stack was finalized after a careful analysis of our requirements versus the availability of resources, keeping our timelines in perspective.

What traffic did you plan this for?

Our platform has been planned for about 200 B2B users and about 2–3 lakh students.

What will your deployment strategy be?

Our application will be deployed on cloud (Azure). There will be no on-premises installations.

What are your engineering practices?

Our developers use GitHub for version control. Separate environments are set up for staging and production. The developers deploy the code from their local environments to staging, and once we test and approve, the code is deployed to production.

What was the hardest technical problem your tech team has solved?

Till date, the most challenging part of the implementation was translating the Excel document into our visualizations.

Once a company has reached the stage to be able to invest in an MVP, the call to action is about aligning every tech step and expense to business. In such a case, the next step of analysis becomes important, and Exhibit 5.2 is a framework for it, used by our tech partner DoodleBlue.[2]

EXHIBIT 5.2   Platform Assessment and Diagnostics

General Questions

1. What has already been achieved and where the startup wants to be in future (a business plan with a sharp focus on technology)? This is important to understand the business objective, technology, and scale of the startup.
2. List any external third-party tools/algorithms/cloud solutions/payment gateways/SMS gateways, etc., used in the existing products.
3. Does your company use any cloud solutions? If yes, please elaborate the service used and the reasons for choosing this particular service.
4. Please share the repository access of the code or send us the code dump.

---

[2] Based on EDUGILD Technology Diagnostic Assessment Report Tool.

Network Security Information

Has your organization ever been compromised (internally or externally)?	
List all the IP address blocks registered to your organization.	
Does your organization use a local firewall(s)? If so, please list quantity and manufacturer(s) of the firewall(s).	
Does your organization use a local intrusion detection system(s) (IDS)?	
Does your organization use a local intrusion prevention system(s) (IPS)?	
If your organization uses local IDS, do you use "host-based" IDS (HIDS) or "network-based" IDS (NIDS) or a combination of both? List the quantity of IDS (both HIDS and NIDS) and IPS devices as well as the manufacturer(s).	
Does your organization have any dedicated connections to other organizations' networks (vendors, business partners)? If so, please list all dedicated connections to other networks.	
Does your organization use any remote access services? Specifically, what type of remote access services does your organization use (VPN or dial-up)?	

Session Security

Does your system have a provision for security, reliability, and confidentiality of data through the use of encryption technology, SSL, or similar session confidentiality protection mechanisms?	
Does the system have controls to ensure that the password is encrypted at the user end so that employees of the organization cannot view it at any point of time?	

System Information

What enterprise resource planning (ERP) application(s) does your organization use (e.g., SAP, PeopleSoft, Oracle, JD Edwards)? Please include a brief description of each.	
What database technologies does your organization use (e.g., Oracle, Microsoft SQL, IBM Db2, MySQL)? Please include a brief description of the purpose of each.	
Elaborate on the storage solutions used—NoSQL (MongoDB, Redis, etc.) or relational (MySQL, PostgreSQL, etc.).	
Does your company make use of an in-memory database? If yes, please elaborate on the usage.	

Service Information

What services do you expose to the Internet (e.g., web, database, FTP, SSH, etc.)?	
What type of authentication do you use for your web services (e.g., Pubcookie, Windows Integrated, .htaccess, etc.)?	
What languages do you use for your web services (e.g., PHP, Perl, Ruby, ASP, etc.)?	
What antivirus application(s) do you use?	
Is your antivirus application implemented using a "managed" client/server architecture, or in a stand-alone configuration?	

Backup and Recovery Procedures

Does the organization have a documented backup policy?	
Are the backup procedures documented?	
Are the backup logs being maintained and are the backups being verified and tested?	
Are the backup media stored safely in line with the risk involved?	
Are there any recovery procedures and have they been tested?	
Are backups of the system-generated audit trails, activity logs, and alert logs maintained as per the documented backup policy?	

DevOps Information

Please elaborate on the below-mentioned points, if applicable:

Code collaboration and version maintenance	
Exception monitoring	
Performance monitoring	
Log management	
Cloud monitoring	
Productivity tools	
Project management tools	
JS build tools/JS task runners	
Business intelligence tools	
Big data tools	

SEO Audit

Check	Observation
How many pages are indexed by Google?	
When you do a site search, does the homepage come up first?	
Does the site have an index bloat?	
Are there any specific crawl issues?	
Does the site have mirror sites?	
If the site uses mirror sites to reduce server load, are the mirrors non-indexed?	
Does the site have an xml sitemap (or sitemaps with an index)?	
Does the xml sitemap follow proper xml protocol?	

Are the sitemaps clean?	
Are the URLs duplicated in the sitemap?	
Is a link to the site's xml sitemap or sitemap index in robots.txt?	
Have the sitemaps been submitted to Google and Bing?	
Does the site have separate sitemaps for the main categories/sections of the website?	
Does the site have an RSS feed?	
Do you have query parameters being indexed?	
Are there errors in the robots. txt file?	
Do you have excluded pages that should not have featured in robots.txt?	
Are there pages/directories that should be included in robots.txt?	
Are there any pages with a no-follow tag?	
Does the site offer print pages?	
If the site offers print pages, do the print pages use CSS or unique URLs?	
If the site offers print pages with unique URLs, are these pages blocked by search engines?	
Does the site use a revisit-after tag?	
If the site is a blog, does it use a plug-in to ping the search engines to let it know it is updated?	

During onboarding, the companies were given 1–2 weeks to frame their responses. One real-life response is shown here.

Questionnaire

The following questionnaire is required to be filled to guarantee the accuracy of the IT audit. Please fill out as much information as possible.

General Questions[3]

1. What has already been achieved and where the startup wants to be in future (a business plan with a sharp focus on technology)? It is important for DoodleBlue to understand the business objective, technology, and scale of the startup.

   - Edvantics is a B2B2C analytics platform for the education domain.
   - The initial focus is on the higher education sector.
   - MVP is analytics as a service for educational institutes.
   - Student platform is currently under development.
   - Edvantics' vision is to create an AI-powered student and learning analytics platform that provides timely insights to equip all the benefactors in an academic life cycle to make faster and better decisions.

2. List any external third-party tools/algorithms/cloud solutions/ payment gateways/SMS gateways, etc. used in the existing products.
   Amazon SES—for sending emails.
   Azure—the server instance is hosted in Azure.

---

[3] These questions have been provided by our tech partners such as DoodleBlue.

Razorpay payment gateway; cPanel.net—not in use anymore, but our original setup was done using this, so the files are present on our server.

3. Please provide details on the tech expertise of the employees/ co-founders.

Our co-founders come with 12+ years of global experience in high-tech and data analytics background. The current platform is being developed through an outsourced vendor and one in-house employee (UI development). Interviews are in progress for more hires.

4. Does your company use any cloud solutions? If yes, please elaborate the service used and the reasons for choosing this particular service.

The company uses Azure for deploying its solution. Azure was chosen as the company had been accepted for Microsoft's BizSpark program and was awarded cloud credits for up to one year.

5. Please share the repository access of the code or send us the code dump. This can be shared.

Network Security Information

Has your organization ever been compromised (internally or externally)?	The servers have never seen any such attack.
List all the IP address blocks registered to your organization.	Currently none.
Does your organization use a local firewall(s)? If so, please list quantity and manufacturer(s) of the firewall(s).	Not yet, but we need to install a firewall, starting with WordPress security plug-ins, such as Sucuri, Wordfence, All-In-One, and SHIELD Security, and later on move onto better firewall mechanisms.

Does your organization use a local intrusion detection system(s) (IDS)?	No
Does your organization use a local intrusion prevention system(s) (IPS)?	No
If your organization uses local IDS, do you use "host-based" IDS (HIDS) or "network-based" IDS (NIDS) or a combination of both? List the quantity of IDS (both HIDS and NIDS) and IPS devices as well as the manufacturer(s).	No
Does your organization have any dedicated connections to other organizations' networks (vendors, business partners)? If so, please list all dedicated connections to other networks.	No
Does your organization use any remote access services? Specifically, what type of remote access services does your organization use (VPN or dial-up)?	We are accessing our servers using SSH & FTP.

Session Security

Does your system have a provision for security, reliability, and confidentiality of data through the use of encryption technology, SSL, or similar session confidentiality protection mechanisms?	We have SSL certificates installed on web servers. (The staging site's certificate has expired, the live site certificate is valid.)

Does the system have controls to ensure that the password is encrypted at the user end so that employees of the organization cannot view it at any point of time?	No

System Information

What ERP application(s) does your organization use (e.g., SAP, PeopleSoft, Oracle, JD Edwards)? Please include a brief description of each.	None as of today
What database technologies does your organization use (e.g., Oracle, Microsoft SQL, IBM Db2, MySQL)? Please include a brief description of the purpose of each.	MySQL v5.6.35
Elaborate on the storage solutions used—NoSQL (MongoDB, Redis, etc.) or relational (MySQL, PostgreSQL, etc.).	MySQL v5.6.35—Relational database solution for the application. Better suited for applications built with LAMP setup.
Does your company make use of in-memory database. If yes, please elaborate on the usage.	No

Service Information

What services do you expose to the Internet (e.g., web, database, FTP, SSH, etc.)?	FTP, SSH, web

What type of authentication do you use for your web services (e.g., Pubcookie, Windows Integrated, .htaccess, etc.)?	No web services
What languages do you use for your web services (e.g., PHP, Perl, Ruby, ASP, etc.)?	PHP
What antivirus application(s) do you use?	None
Is your antivirus application implemented using a "managed" client/server architecture, or in a stand-alone configuration?	NA

Backup and Recovery Procedures

Does the organization have a documented backup policy?	No, but as a general rule, we take backups of the code and database on every production release.
Are the backup procedures documented?	No
Are the backup logs being maintained and are the backups being verified and tested?	No
Are the backup media stored safely in line with the risk involved?	No
Are there any recovery procedures and have they been tested?	No
Are backups of the system-generated audit trails, activity logs, and alert logs maintained as per the documented backup policy?	No

DevOps Information

Please elaborate on the below-mentioned points, if applicable:

Code collaboration and version maintenance	Local version control using Git
Exception monitoring	Log files of web and database servers
Performance monitoring	No
Log management	No
Cloud monitoring	No
Productivity tools	No
Project management tools	No
JS build tools/JS task runners	NA
Business intelligence tools	No
Big data tools	NA

SEO Audit

Even though we have done our groundwork in digital marketing (SEO, Google AdWords, lead generation channels, and content), currently we are not very active on the digital marketing front. However, we do have a digital marketing strategy in place, which we hope to execute as soon as we have our content and relevant website nailed down.

Check	Observation
How many pages are indexed by Google?	NA
When you do a site search, does the homepage come up first?	NA
Does the site have an index bloat?	NA
Are there any specific crawl issues?	NA
Does the site have mirror sites?	No
If the site uses mirror sites to reduce server load, are the mirrors non-indexed?	NA

Check	Observation
Does the site have an xml sitemap (or sitemaps with an index)?	No
Does the xml sitemap follow proper xml protocol?	NA
Are the sitemaps clean?	NA
Are the URLs duplicated in the sitemap?	NA
Is a link to the site's xml sitemap or sitemap index in robots.txt?	NA
Have the sitemaps been submitted to Google and Bing?	No
Does the site have separate sitemaps for the main categories/sections of the website?	NA
Does the site have an RSS feed?	No
Do you have query parameters being indexed?	NA
Are there errors in the robots.txt file?	NA
Do you have excluded pages that should not have featured in robots.txt?	NA
Are there pages/directories that should be included in robots.txt?	NA
Are there any pages with a no-follow tag?	NA
Does the site offer print pages?	Yes
If the site offers print pages, do the print pages use CSS or unique URLs?	CSS
If the site offers print pages with unique URLs, are these pages blocked by search engines?	NA
Does the site use a revisit-after tag?	NA
If the site is a blog, does it use a plug-in to ping the search engines to let it know it is updated?	NA

This filled-in questionnaire throws up a number of blanks as well. It is clearly evident that a thorough technology roadmap discussion needs more inputs than what the founders may have thought about. It is all about getting the right information in one place and linking it to a scalable business.

Product as a Resource

The best way to start this section is to read about the journey of UpGrad—a company co-founded by Ronnie Screwvala.

SPOTLIGHT: UpGrad[4]

UpGrad is an online higher education company that "builds careers of tomorrow." Partnering with academic institutions on the one side and leading corporates on the other, UpGrad creates online programs in areas that traditional education does not cater to sufficiently, particularly in the areas of data, technology, and digital. UpGrad offers its programs on mobile and desktop platforms and enables mentoring and career support along with digital-first content and networking opportunities to create a holistic learning experience.

The Founders

UpGrad has an experienced founding team that has worked on education businesses across the globe. The co-founder, Ronnie Screwvala, before starting UpGrad, pioneered cable TV in India through his conglomerate UTV, which he sold to Disney at an enterprise value of $2 billion. His co-founder Mayank has led education investment and consulting for more than 12 years across India, Latin America, Africa, and Southeast Asia. I, the third co-founder, advised Bertelsmann,

---

[4] Based on inputs from UpGrad head Marius Westhoff, who is a close friend.

Europe's largest media and education conglomerate, for several years on investments in digital media and education across Europe and India before joining UpGrad's founding team in March 2015.

The UpGrad Genesis

Ever since the Internet became mainstream in the early 2000s, online education was one of the first areas that many players tried to conquer. From Moodle, to Coursera, Udemy, Khan Academy, and many more, online education created an opportunity to offer learning opportunities for millions. While all of these companies made a big impact and became pioneers in their fields, we felt that many players tried to replicate an offline experience in an online environment rather than looking at learning from a digital-first angle— as though the concept of learning were invented in the digital era.

With that ambition and vision in mind—to enable individuals to reach their full professional potential through the most engaging, digital-first learning experience—we started UpGrad in March 2015. At that point in time, the *gross enrollment ratio* of India (i.e., the number of college-aged professionals who are actually going to college) was at 20–25 percent. At the same time, economies such as the US (70% +), Europe (60% +), and China (35% +) were much ahead when it came to the gross enrollment ratio. It was evident that India had to catch up. However, doing so by means of brick-and-mortar education centers would have required investments far beyond $80 billion. So in order to bridge that gap, India had to find alternative solutions, and we all believed that the online platform could play a key part in solving this problem.

Ever since we started in March 2015, we grew from a team of 5 to 170 across Mumbai and Bangalore. We have built partnerships with institutions such as BITS Pilani, International Institute of Information Technology (IIIT) Bangalore, and Mudra Institute of Communications Ahmedabad (MICA) to offer digital-first certification and diploma programs. Through our paid programs, we have so far educated around 3,000 students. We have been able to generate course completion rates of +88 percent for our online programs and see strong customer satisfaction across courses. Our free-for-all StartUp India Learning Program, launched in collaboration with the Government of India, has so far trained more than 170,000 Indians on how to start their business and become employers themselves.

Have Some Clarity on What Your Product Should Look Like

As mentioned before, from day one, we were clear that we wanted to create a digital-first learning experience and reinvent education, as though it were invented in 2015. Most players in the market were very strong in one domain—either they were delivering a strong service element, they were strong at content creation, or they had built a great technology platform or learning management system (LMS). We felt that in order to provide effective digital learning, you cannot look at only content, technology, or services, you have to look at all three aspects together and create a holistic experience. Let me give you an idea of what that means to us in these three categories.

- *Technology:* From a technology perspective, most of the LMS systems that we had seen were supporting a one-sided interaction between the platform and the individual, wherein a learner could go through content (i.e., videos or text) on an online platform and he/she could then answer pre-defined questions on the platform itself and see automated scores. Now close your eyes, think of your college days, and ask yourself: "Who did I interact with the most? Who helped me with my assignments? Who helped me if I was not sure about a certain concept? Who would I exchange ideas with?" I am pretty sure the answer would not be your teacher or your teaching associate, but rather your buddy, your fellow student, your college mate. We really felt that the existing LMS platforms were lacking one fundamental component of learning— the peer-to-peer interaction. This is what we wanted to facilitate in our learning platform—peer-to-peer learning and interaction. To facilitate this, we built many features into our technology platform: discussion forums, focused group discussions, poll questions, group assignments, and many more such features that allow students to work together and learn from each other. Also, next to the P2P elements, we made sure from day one that we have some idea of how to scale any of the features that we built into our product. While initially after launching the product, one can improvise and fix non-scalable processes through short-term hacks, we were clear that in the long term, there will have to be a scalable solution to these features; otherwise, it would not make sense to launch them.

- *Content:* From a content perspective, we felt that most online education programs and providers were trying to replicate an offline experience—positioning a professor in front of a whiteboard or green wall, recording his/her lecture, and hosting a 20–30 minute video on an online platform, hoping that students will engage with this type of content, with the result that they dropped off in masses—and completion rates between 2 percent and 40 percent are still very common. We believed that content has to be engaging, as we are de facto competing with Facebook, YouTube, Instagram, and other such media for the attention span of our users. That is why we have built a team of content strategists, instruction design educators as well as creative directors and executive producers with a media background in order to create engaging content, bite-sized into 3–4 minute video chunks, interspersed with engaging elements such as in-video questions in order to keep the learner involved throughout. We use different elements for our content—from rich case studies, which give the learner a feeling of "diving" into a business situation, to interactive discussions between faculty members and industry professionals, to lectures and virtual coding bootcamps. The content tries to break through the stereotype of online lectures and keeps the user engaged through the entire learning experience.

- *Services:* From a services perspective, we felt that we can simply not expect anyone to know how to learn online without some handholding and some guidance through the journey. Most of our customers and all of us from the initial team at UpGrad have had experiences of only the brick-and-mortar university system, where we sat in a classroom listening to a professor. Expecting an individual who has never used the online mode before to just adapt to it without any support, no matter how intuitive the platform may be, was something we did not think would work. That is why we introduced the concept of student mentors across all our programs. Every student has a dedicated mentor, whose sole responsibility is to ensure that the student stays engaged with the program and is happy with the overall experience. The student mentor can be reached at any time and is available to handhold the student throughout his/ her journey. Next to the student mentor, a set of teaching assistants and industry experts are available to solve any academic doubts that the student may have. Offline events help the students to build strong communities and network with each other, while alumni and external grading experts help in providing feedback to the assessments and assignments set throughout the program.

We believe that this holistic view on digital-first education, across technology, content, and services is something that will help tremendously in order to build a meaningful education experience. And we were clear about these three facets from day one.

Talk to Customers and Create a Product that Makes Them Happy

No matter how much clarity you may have from day one, do not ever make the mistake of thinking that you will be able to build the perfect product in one go. A good product experience for the customer requires a lot of iterations and a lot of review and redevelopment. We continuously talk to all our customers and students, especially the ones who report issues or give us low ratings (in the content ratings for each session). These student insights help us to rebuild our programs, add product features that are meaningful, and adjust content where needed. On an average, we redevelop around 25 percent of our content every academic year to ensure that all programs are up-to-date and meet customer requirements. Being close to the users and hearing them out is something that is key to our organization and key to the way we develop programs at UpGrad.

Conclusion

Have a good idea and a strong vision of how the user experience will be before you start. Carefully studying competitors' products and identifying product differentiators through detailed user interviews helped us a lot in defining and refining our offering. Being open to customer feedback and adjusting the product by eliminating errors helped us to raise our internal bar and improve customer satisfaction remarkably over the years—*the most unhappy customers are the ones that you can derive the most insights from.*

Product Development and Management

The journey of moving from an idea in the mind to creating a sustainable business is a challenging one. It is like a house of cards that needs to be balanced, and, in turn, there has to be just the adequate amount of adhesive to create a strong product management and product life cycle roadmap. Many startups do not realize that simultaneously as the product strategy is being mapped to competitive edge, the entire product life cycle should be planned in order to

1. counter the anticipated moves of competition,
2. stay ahead of future competition, and
3. ensure the product starts to evolve as a cash cow or star.

There are strong misconceptions about what product management is all about, which leads to the myth that having an MVP or a PMF (product-market fit) is the stage to stop. Due to this thought process, startups sometimes desist from hiring the best product management minds, since they are not aware of the importance of this *indispensable and critical activity*.

The wrong milestones of "product readiness" can lead to startups wasting a lot of time and effort on something called a "white lie start", which happens when a half-baked product is perceived as being ready, primarily because the startup's management is not able to communicate the product expectations to the product managers. In other words, a product life cycle management roadmap must be laid with enough lead-time for the teams to deliberate and create something viable and launch ready. This is with a view on not just the present but the expected evolutions of the future as well—being a leader is the only way to be successful before the followers catch up.

The foundation of the creation of a product/service needs to be rock solid, and is the cornerstone of how a startup can become a flourishing organization. Developing the startup's baby (the product/service) is everyone's responsibility, because at stake is the company's success as seen by internal as well as external stakeholders.

The core of the startup business is the capability of translating an idea into a product or a solution that focuses on a definitive and significant need gap felt by consumers. The product management function is the key to achieving excellence in product creation and all the product life cycle processes, which in turn are crucial for the success of any startup.

Another important factor contributing to the success of a startup is exactly being sure of "Do we know exactly what to build?" This will cover a series of core questions for the startup:

- What to build?
- Whom to build for?
- Why will consumers use it?
- When will consumers use it?

A successful organization creates a process that institutionalizes the answers to these questions, and integrates this process with the product development process. Competence in primary research techniques helps uncover consumer opportunities and gaps from the answers to these questions. The competence and discipline of such consumer-oriented product development needs to be formalized under a product management team.

Product management is the art and science of the new-product creation process that inculcates customer focus in the entire organization. This function owns the product roadmap as well as the product vision of the organization. It should be the aspiration of every startup to reach the next level of competitiveness, for which the utility of the product/service to the consumers is critical.

Since the product management function is the backbone of the product development process, it is important to understand the challenges and fallouts that occur when this function is being established and evolved, along with guidance on what it takes to face these challenges, because they will always exist—one can only minimize their impact.

Product development is a series of activities that incorporates conceptualization, design, development, and marketing of the newly created goods or services. Core product development broadly involves the following four steps and uses various techniques to accomplish these:

1. *Discover* what the consumer needs through detailed primary research.
2. *Define* the solution that best solves the problem through iterative checks.
3. *Design* the complete user experience across the solution.
4. *Develop* the final solution and prepare it for a GTM handing over.

Idea generation is the systematic search for a new solution concept to cater to the already identified significant need gap of the consumers. This moves into the *idea screening* stage, in which all the recommended solution concepts are tested against clear parameters in order to select one that will be developed into a business proposition. A business analysis of the new product concept maps the revenue potential against the business costs to arrive at the profit potential. Once the startup has arrived at a confident business plan through the described process, actual product development starts through an iterative test-marketing and improvement process. The iterative test-marketing process develops the product toward a full-scale commercial launch of the business.

Product management leads and owns the aforementioned four steps and integrates the optimum consumer solution.

Product development begins with mapping the solution idea against the consumer need gap. It then analyzes the market and competitive offerings available to create a differentiated product vision. The key factor is to deliver a unique offering based on customer needs.

The product development role spans a wide range of activities—from strategic to tactical. As a process, it is the central gear among the sales, marketing, operations, support, and engineering functions. Product management must involve cross-functional leadership to bring together these different organizational functions. This can be done by creating a transparent prioritization framework for all product and feature developments.

Product management needs to marry good business under-standing with strong technology domain knowledge. This allows product development to remain agile to continuously plan, execute, and improve the product. At the very core, the startup needs to have a champion of the consumer's cause who can drive the end-to-end product development process for the organization.

A company that I started advising in March 2016, Gradopedia, has one of the most mature founders at a very young age. The company's product management journey has been astounding, although a bit overcautious. I have watched the company for the past 18 months now and they are steadily gaining popularity (Exhibit 5.3).

EXHIBIT 5.3   A Journey of Pivot and Scaleup

Gradopedia Had a Product Evolution Experience to AmbitionUp[5]

"Hitesh we're not sure about how this market will play out or what needs to be done to solve this problem. Our decision to induct you does not mean a decision to induct your company, current product stage, or your business plan—it's only you."

While Hitesh, the founder, had a mixed reaction, the possibility of an accelerator believing in their vision was surreal—he had been worried, confused, and mostly panicking every night, and getting lesser hours of sleep as the nights went by.

Something about the size of the opportunity gave the team of Gradopedia, rechristened to AmbitionUp, the right amount of confidence and focus to discover what might solve the employability problem, and what they could do together as a company.

AmbitionUp provides employability mapping services. It works as a job seeker's personal guide to help them become more employable.

First Weekend of the EDUGILD Program

While AmbitionUp was interacting with different mentors to establish its vision, they got a huge push in the form of Manish Upadhyay—a fellow edtech entrepreneur, co-founder of Liqvid, and a strategic advisor to EDUGILD. Manish was

---

[5] Based on inputs from Hitesh Awtaney, Founder and CEO, AmbitionUp.

as passionate about assessments and skills as Hitesh was passionate about helping job seekers find their ideal fit. While Hitesh was taking Manish through their user feedback and gap analysis, he shared his thoughts on how assessments are a huge barrier. Talented candidates were not having a good recruitment experience on competitors' platforms. In turn, it was leading to frustration which recruiters had to experience before finally meeting someone they may remotely like.

And within the 45-minute discussion, Manish outlined that assessments could be a great category, given how careers were changing and people with expertise in only one area were finding it difficult to hire others. That insight combined with AmbitionUp's ability to curate videos and content on new careers would then go on to be the differentiator in a crowded yet underserved market.

Second Weekend of the EDUGILD Program

The MD of one of the biggest recruitment agencies comes over; the air conditioner in the room was not the reason why Hitesh was shivering so much—it was the fear of the MD mentioning something that may make no sense to him. The MD went through Hitesh's entire presentation and said one thing: "Hitesh all this is good, but when the hiring managers or recruiters are looking for someone urgently, and the functional managers are putting pressure to hire, how does the HR team manage to be selective enough?"

While there was no immediate answer back then, Hitesh made a note of this remark, and today the platform has integrated a predictability score—an employer can see in real time how selective they could be and how many aspirants would be eligible to apply. It gives them the confidence of setting a benchmark based on the actual available talent pool as compared to multiple trial-and-error techniques, using which they would either have to wait until the right talent applied or spend time going through irrelevant applications.

Solving Complex Problems with Design
EDUGILD is probably the only accelerator focused on design as a service provided to startups. So, once Hitesh knew what he wanted to build, he got in touch with our internal design team, a young lot of independent designers and interns. Their questions were far more complex than ever witnessed, each grilling AmbitionUp's purpose of existence but at the same time ensuring that AmbitionUp would stand out in the way their platform worked. Hitesh remembers answering questions such as "If AmbitionUp were a person, what would they be wearing?" A designer tried to gauge how they wanted people to feel every time they entered the company name in their address bar, and Hitesh answered, "She could be wearing a simple and casual jumpsuit." And then there was a 3-hour discussion on what the four primary colors representing the company identity would be, along with other colors that would form a part of the palette.

As the questions became more targeted, reviewing the path and journey a seeker would take throughout the platform, we soon realized how it could personalize their experience even before they asked for it!

The platform at present is more effective than all competitors combined, only because the design team asked the toughest questions, cared more than anyone about the UI experience, and finally because EDUGILD really believes in the value of design.

Shortly after the entire process and design were in place, it was inferred that solving with design would indeed become the core value throughout the company and that it would be ensured that the service would be made more functional than ever. Today, the company invests the same amount of thought and rigor while designing a banner image, and it is only because they have seen what design can do and how it is the easiest way to show users that AmbitionUp cares more than any other platform does.

Making Careers Tangible, Searchable, Trackable and the Next Steps

Job seekers take anywhere between 1 and 3 months to find the job that matches all their criteria. Some stick on to the jobs they pick up, others look at them confused and dazed, the alternate options seeming to be as perplexing as the one they have currently picked.

On the AmbitionUp platform, aspirants take out 2 minutes, get matched with all possible careers, and get an indication about which ones fit them the best personally—no two aspirants get the same fitment! Next, the platform gives them a view of what happens at an average day at work, which allows them to look at the career from a realistic perspective even before they have applied for a single job or spoken to any company. Their ability to pick and pursue a career, look ahead at the next steps, and plan exactly what they need to do to become more employable is something that really excites them (and the founders) about using the platform.

Hitesh is clear that there is a future version of this story that describes how AmbitionUp can help channelize the country's youth, making them more focused toward their goals, and how aspirants do not need to blindly listen to their parents, relatives, or neighbors while choosing their careers. We will soon live in a time when our career choice will be driven by a culmination of insights from all the people who have ever had a professional career, and the services offered by AmbitionUp will be equivalent to that support system—*guiding people to be more focused and excited about selecting careers that personally work for them.*

Learning from the experiences of founders and their product and tech journeys, let us now create a product management framework for startups to fit their processes into.

1. Do the founders and core team members understand product management and its evolution as well as the progress of a product life cycle right from introduction to decline and the concept of extending the life cycle?
2. Does the startup have a product management vertical? If yes, then have the founders taken charge of product management or has a manager been hired for it, or is it outsourced? If a manager has been hired, how has her/his capability to form a part of this important team been assessed?
3. What have been the founders' learnings and success stories in the journey of creating the product and what is the thought behind the market fit of the current product and future roadmap development?
4. What parameters will define the success or failure of the product management initiatives? What checks and balances will ensure

that there is utmost consistency in the product management strategy and its execution?

5. How has it been ensured that the product management planning is consistent throughout the management team and internal and external stakeholders?

6. How would the founders define the most important difference made in a product by the product management team?

   a. Technology
   b. UI/UX
   c. Shape/size
   d. Cost
   e. Scalability/niche
   f. Monetization

7. While creating the team of co-founders, did the primary founder passionately select partner/s with a knack for product management and assign to them the task of chief product officer (CPO)?

8. Is there a scientific scale to measure the success of the product, taking into account the following parameters?

   a. Technology
   b. Sales and marketing
   c. Execution and implementation
   d. Customer support
   e. Partners' development
   f. Journey to the status of star/cash cow

Element of Cluelessness

It has been around two years since my interaction with startups began, and I would have dealt with at least 1,000 until now. In my experience, there are greater gaps in the product management strategy of soft-tech companies than that of product-oriented startups. The critical development of the product management function, deploying state-of-the-art tools and techniques, and product management operations, seems to be more a need-based evolution than a well-thought-through path in soft-tech companies.

A product group and its leader (who may be the startup founder or core team member initially) is like the MD of the product vertical. This makes her/him responsible for all the aspects of the product—creation, launch, success, failure, etc. A product lead has to focus extensively on the product and everything else connected to it. This can be development, implementation, training, service, life cycle, marketing, and sales amongst others. The product management team must decide how to delegate the responsibilities of and/or time spent on each of these important functions—in-house resource or outsource. There are very critical and close-to-the-heart decisions involved in this activity. For example, if your startup has a web-based service, then the product owners need to decide whether to create the entire snowball in-house or out-source the concept development and creation. With outsourcing come the considerations of protecting intellectual property (IP) or the original idea, quality control, and time to market, aspects that need to be finely balanced by the product management system.

The Customer's Heart Must Be Kept Beating

It is important that product evolution always address a customer requirement, else it becomes a research project, not one that will be remembered for a long time to come. Product managers work on a T model—the horizontal line indicates exploring the width of the concept of the product while the vertical line indicates going deep down into the features, one at a time, and designing the most suitable market fit.

Product development and management often suffer from the syndrome of learning that founders and product teams bring from their background of experience in other companies or startups— sometimes they try to superimpose the concepts they have learnt in the past since they have seen them being implemented practically. They fail to realize that superimposing their past learnings with other companies on their own product strategy may not necessarily bring the desired results.

It is important for each startup to understand that their product management is never going to be an emulation of anyone else's simulation of product management, and each time they consider the product strategy, a tailor-made effort will be needed, since every startup has its own vision and approach.

As the CEO, the company founder/s cannot completely neglect any single function of their company. "I'll just focus on public relations; I'm not going to worry about financing at all" simply will not work. So too must a product manager focus on *all* aspects of the product.

In order to cover the entire scope of the product, the product manager serves each member of the management team in a supporting role. Specifically, product managers help each area maintain a sharper focus. For example, to support the marketing team, the product manager ensures that the collaterals, product positioning, and conversations with the press sharpen their focus on product success, benefits, and capabilities. Product management becomes the link between the top-level goals set at the strategic level and obtaining results that truly reflect those goals. This extra set of hands becomes a vital catalyst for the company's growth, as it extends beyond the ability of each vice president to micromanage his/her operations.

This leads to the discussion of an important aspect—product releases. The product management team defines a company's release schedule and approach. It ensures that all the processes involved are developed based on well-known consumer requirements, and will lead up to the right first impression on a consumer and result in actual sales after the product launch.

Exhibit 5.4 is a brief description of the company enhancement and reorientation experienced by ClassBoat followed by the linking of their product evolution process to their business. Clearly, they accomplished a brilliant market fit and the results are in line.

EXHIBIT 5.4 ClassBoat: Turning Passion into an Opportunity

Jay and Renu, a husband and wife team, are the founders of ClassBoat, a successful career-building and learning portal. Together, they have over 20 years of experience combining a variety of backgrounds such as management, consulting, and technology, spanning 12 countries.

Renu comes from an education background, as her parents are both teachers. Jay grew up with a mother who was an entrepreneur herself and built a strong matrimonial portal. Since the beginning, they have both been interested in becoming entrepreneurs and have been passionate about creating a large transnational impact that will benefit the society and economy. With this passion and mission in mind, they landed in India two years back from London and have been working ever since toward building their ClassBoat business.

Since landing in India two years ago, they were consistently on the lookout for areas in which they could create a significant social and economic impact. They observed that while there were many talented people who had the expertise, capacity, and credibility in their specific talent, they did not know how to market it to benefit themselves financially. They realized that this problem exists on a large scale and affects the personal and economic growth of millions of individuals. They decided to dive deeper into the matter and carry out further research, and observed the following:

1. The "rat race" was no longer just about everyone becoming an engineer or doctor, anymore.
2. Increase in the middle-class income increased their affordability index.
3. Parents are now keen on exploring their children's interests and hobbies.
4. Alternative career choices are being explored by working professionals. The society has transformed to accept and respect these alternative careers.

For thousands of educators in India, outside the academic sector, teaching some kind of skills or hobbies, trying to get students can become a nightmarish process. With so many avenues for marketing classes, such as, Facebook, Twitter, websites, newspaper ads, and so on, it can become overwhelming. So, it is not uncommon to find an educator, offering coaching classes, for example, but having a tough time finding the students to fill their classroom.

With the confidence gained from their research and their complimentary skills, they felt that they could confidently embark on this entrepreneurial venture. They felt financially secure to see it through, even if it would be difficult for the first few years. Thus, began their journey with ClassBoat.

ClassBoat reduces the educator's time to revenue by curating the learners they need, which is what they charge for. They are driving this solution through technology. The scope is limitless, unbound by geography, and scalable.

Once an educator decides to list their classes on ClassBoat, they can sit back, relax, and focus on doing what they love—teaching their skill/talent to students. Their market presence will increase, which means that they will get more students in their class and thus increased revenue. The pay-as-you-go packages make it easy for them to keep track of how many students are filling up in their class; they can top up the amount in their account, which gets depleted with every candidate lead they accept. So, the only thing they have to do is respond to the leads of students interested in their classes via the emails and SMSs we send to them.

Eight months after having started, ClassBoat got selected by EDUGILD and received seed funding, which gave them the boost they needed. They grew from

- 2 to 16 people
- 500 to 7000 educators, and mostly all top educational institutes in Pune are using ClassBoat's services for acquiring students
- 500 to 25,000 leads per month
- ₹20,000 per month to ₹700,000 per month in revenue (nearing profit-making every month)

Today, ClassBoat has created a niche market in the area by offering services like none before, such as the following:

- They curate learners as nobody has ever done. They curate seriousness.
- Until date, no one has tried to create a career-building platform.
- Their other features are

  ○ *Lead buyback policy.* If the leads do not meet the client's standards, ClassBoat will offer refund by way of a buyback. The refund reflects in the client's top-up account.

  ○ *Three-way verification.* Each lead goes through three stages of personal and technology-oriented verification before reaching the client.

  ○ *Quality assurance* of leads is provided.

- At present, they call each learner for a three-way verification, which they will soon replace with chatbot technology.

With the company growing and doing well, they want to drive the organization to its next potential level, creating career trends and aligning educators before anybody else can make it happen. When it comes to career building or learning, ClassBoat wants to strive to be constantly ahead of the curve across the nation, and hopefully globally one day.

Ultimately the potential to operate in a dynamically changing environment, often without resources and support, is what defines a startup, which has a direct correlation to product evolution.

CHAPTER 6

Developing the Organization: Founders as Flag Bearers

In my experience, I have found developing organizations for startups quite challenging. The biggest contributing factor I have observed is the inevitable differences of opinions that crop up among the founders, leading to organizational instability. So, with a weak foundation, the castle begins to shake in no time.

Choosing a startup co-founder is difficult enough; further, to keep their faith alive in order to retain them for a substantial period of time is no cakewalk. Now imagine the implications of a co-founder/core team member leaving or the startup realizing that they are not a good fit for the organization. Are early-stage companies equipped to handle a co-founder's sudden exit or to manage a situation in which they have to ask one to exit? It is very important to be aware of the decisions and steps that must be taken by company initiators to safeguard the continuity and value of the startup under such circumstances while maintaining a sharp focus on their main objectives.

Organizational development hiccups happen initially at the founder level. At this stage, core team members and/or founders can choose to leave the company for a variety of reasons. I saw this happening at MuseIn, YoScholar, and TinyTapps. The matter becomes unmanageable due to the timing and nature of the exit, which can generally be classified as follows:

- *Exit due to uncertain future:* Consider YoScholar, for example, where the core team split before the company product could be launched due to a disagreement among the members—one part of the team wanted to do something that the other members did not agree to. Such exits are also possible due to family reasons, illnesses, or a better opportunity available outside. In the case of MuseIn, the co-founder was offered a very lucrative corporate opportunity that was too good to give up. In such situations, people make the obvious choice, and this nature of exit is the hardest to deal with, simply because it comes with very little warning. So, in the case of MuseIn, the co-founders pitched to EDUGILD jointly, and, during onboarding, one of them went with a corporate job rather than continue the startup journey. Similarly, the person who pitched TinyTapps to EDUGILD was not seen as a part of the team when the company was accepted to be accelerated.
- *Exit due to differences:* It is not uncommon to see the relationship among co-founders coming under strain due to matters that both sides cannot help. It could be because of a simple communication gap, a misunderstanding, issues with alignment of values and vision, even to the extent of handling investor communication. In mild forms, all these issues have been faced by TinyTapps and YoScholar. However, the exits were not threatening to the business. In such cases, the impact can be minimized by ending the collaboration amicably.

- *Exit by mutual consent:* During the course of starting and scaling up, there can be situations when it is clear that things are not working out—whether it is due to the founders' performance, the need for a different skill set, or some other reason. At such times, it is best to buy out the other person(s)' stakes and sever the relationship.

I have experienced founder deliberations and golden handshakes in a few companies—TinyTapps, YoScholar, MuseIn. While in TinyTapps, the founders disagreed on the way ahead, in YoScholar, the founders started looking at different ways to fulfill short-term needs. However, in the case of MuseIn, a co-founder exited before the company even established itself. When MuseIn pitched to me, I really liked the founders' zeal; they were well sorted and appeared a balanced duo. One of the founders was full time into the venture and the other one had to transition in a few months. After we agreed to work together, the part-time founder went to his workplace to resign. However, he was offered a lucrative proposition to stick around, and it seems the company's offer was too compelling to overlook. So, finally, the founders broke off, and Goutam and I committed to ensure that other co-founder's exit will not affect the company. Today, MuseIn has their share of feedback and direction from Viacom18, Ronnie Screwvala's RSVP, Karan Grover (producer for A. R. Rahman), and many such feathers in their cap. The co-founder's exit is now a thing of the past for them.

These episodes have led me to ensure that I discuss such possibilities with company founders early on and suggest certain actions that are as follows:

1. *Make it formal:* If founders are friends or acquaintances, they usually do not bother to distinguish between their personal

relationship and professional job descriptions. It is very seldom that founder/co-founder agreements are formalized, including exit conditions among other formalities. I recommend that every startup do this on the day of incorporation to avoid collateral damages in the time to come.

2. *Activate your contingency plan:* Depending on the reason for the exit, a "core team member" insurance and backup policy might be needed sooner than later. This is a critical piece of a good contingency plan—something that not just your startup, but also your customers and investors will require. Further, in these circumstances, it is important to let your senses to be overloaded and your partner's work to be delegated to you, at least, on a short-term basis to cover the transition period. This would make you stretch beyond your comfort zone to not just perform but to also figure out the way forward.

3. *Cover all legal angles:* The company founders must make sure that their IP is protected when going through an off-boarding process. The exiting party will have to ensure that their side of obligations/lock-ins and confidentiality agreements are met, including the harsher non-compete clauses if any. In one case, the non-compete clause had to be executed in a company breakup instance and it became a challenge to protect the IP. In another instance, when we were onboarding a particular company, the co-founders split. Moving on, both the sides applied for our favors and ensured that they owned the IP and had better capability to rebuild the organization. While we backed one team, our relationship did not last too long, and we severed the engagement amicably. Every startup must consult a lawyer in order to ensure that the legal risks of severance are not severe and the "divorce" is by mutual consent.

4. *Parley and debate:* In the breakups I have witnessed, a few factors stood out glaringly.

   a. Timing of exit. This is a very important factor and I have seen two particular instances—one in which the severance was based on mutually agreed timing and the other was an abrupt exit. One must be prepared for both situations.

   b. Metamorphosis. This term is sometimes also referred to as transition. If the exiting partner is not going to be available further at all, the handover and transition of all work and relationships have to be done as if it is a matter of life and death.

   c. Ownership boundaries. I have witnessed situations where the exit was a result of the leaving partner relinquishing all ownership, and, in some cases, they became nuisance value. So the rights and ownerships of the exiting person(s) must be legally put in place. This is also associated with the valuation at exit, which can and should be hedged in advance.

   d. Alliance. We have a classic example of this situation in YoScholar where a core team member moved on amicably. However, the alliance never broke off. The exiting core team member is a corporate employee now as well as an equity owner in YoScholar. In addition, he is always available whenever the company needs his guidance and support. It is a dilemma whether a continuing alliance must be captured legally or be left to the goodwill among the founders themselves.

   e. Transparent information to stakeholders. This is seldom seen in the startup system. However, each company must inform its investors and customers about any change in company structure. It is just to ensure that the exiting founder is relieved of the liability, and the continuing members are able to get a full view of the prevalent structure and processes. It is of utmost importance to be proactive in communicating to your customers and investors what is happening with the business and why, so that their faith and confidence in the venture remain unshaken. A change in the company structure should not leave the stakeholders nervous.

Beginning with the first batch of startups I started engaging with, I have kept asking the CEOs/founders about their greatest challenges, and inevitably organization development came up at the highest priority. As an experienced advisor to more than 20 companies, I know that poor HR and organization development skills can sink a promising company or bring it to a standstill. The single largest issue that causes the most heartache in a startup is human resource challenges and the dilemma to delegate or not.

Most startups do not have the bandwidth or money to have a full-time HR resource, and some of them realize the need for it very late. However, if startups put best HR practices into place in the growth phase and make that a discipline, then they would have fewer and fewer issues going forward. I strongly recommend instilling good HR practices in startups at the early stages, and, at EDUGILD, we strive to bring HR specialists to talk to the companies early enough. Also during our startup review meetings, the topic of organization development is regularly raised with the founders and the investors alike.

Organization Development as the Key Element

It is important for startup founders to understand that the human resource function is a core organizational function and not a one-time activity. I say so because many of them come with a mindset of "do it for me" (DIFM) and not "do it myself" from an organizational development standpoint. This is the most important aspect for a startup to be able to become a company. Who would know better about it than Hitesh, the founder of AmbitionUp, who struggled to get the right partners onboard, or for that matter YoScholar, who set up offices in Pune and Delhi, not knowing that it may become an overkill in due course? Raman, the founder of Simulanis, tried all the tricks up his sleeve, right from campus hiring to taking the help of HR consultants. However, at the end of the day, Simulanis gains its aggressive overtures from Raman as the founder.

At many startups, human resources engagement and development is an afterthought; entrepreneurs somehow tend to believe that organizational development is not an urgent problem, and by the time it becomes one, they are not able to find time to figure out solutions. As important as it is to have a proper PMF, so it is also to focus on the organization's fit to the market segment. It is of strategic importance for any startup to hire–acquihire–consult and venture–partner the best people. Startups have to ensure that their organization develops through the following: co-founders, core team members, employees, advisors, and VPs.

Incidentally, in my experience so far, the companies have some insights about co-founders and employees; however, they are quite unaware of developing the company with core team members (ones who come on board with part equity and part revenue share) and VPs who come on sweat equity terms. I always advise my companies to go for retainership-based advisors so that the outcomes and honorariums in return are predictable, which makes the whole engagement serious and time-bound. An example is Ahhaa.com, which has a beautiful VP engagement with Karan Grover. They have fixed milestones to be achieved and vesting of equity agreed against each goalpost. Then we have YoScholar and its advisor who work on a revenue-generation-based partnership. We also have sweat equity VPs who give 20–30 hours each month for building up the startups' journey. So, it is very important for a company to compartmentalize its business and organization evolution with people in all the domains mentioned here. On this note, let's discuss an in-house VP.

SPOTLIGHT: EDUGILD—India's First Edtech Startups Accelerator

EDUGILD is a startups accelerator that supports entrepreneurship in the field of edtech, knowledge management, and learning and development. This initiative has the core objective of nurturing valuable IP and best-in-class ideas that need general guidance and counsel, especially with respect to the course to take for commercialization.

To date, MAEER's MIT Pune, our founding knowledge partner, has created successful brands and professionals in the field of technology, management, design, school education, and healthcare—an experience that puts impeccable credibility behind the accelerator initiative.

To be a step ahead of traditional accelerators, the goal at EDUGILD is to get great ideas off the ground, by first assessing the team that aspires to set up a venture and their capability to pursue the right business instincts. This program is important for the economic development of India, ultimately manifesting at a global level. Beyond physical space and equipment, the initiative provides a very valuable booster for startups. It brings in the necessary business and DTM advice—precisely the sort of knowledge and skills many edtech startups lack. This is furthered by funding the ventures and taking them to a launch platform in the true sense.

EDUGILD's VPs

Entrepreneurial success is not the result of a single person's efforts. There is always a team involved. The team is made up of mentors, subject matter experts (SMEs), institutional partners, investors, working partners, employees, vendors, and clients. All these people play an important role in the success of the enterprise.

VP collaboration is integral to making startups successful, and, in the 21st century world, it is perhaps more relevant. By associating each startup with a core VP, there is alignment of expert opinion and subject matter practitioners, which benefits both sides. This would require VP to be a constant guide to the startup and spend at least 3–4 hours with them (face-to-face or virtually) every week, and participate with EDUGILD on the weekly assessment calls with the startup. At the core level, VP is expected to

- be an all-in-one guide to the startup as a friend and sounding board;
- get 1 percent sweat equity stake;
- have the first right to pick equity in the startup through seed funding;

- help the startup to connect, through the EDUGILD network, with other mentors and resources as required;
- use their own and EDUGILD's network to help the startup to establish customer relationships for proof-of-concept and beta tests;
- critically review the startup's customer insights and user feedback, and realign if required;
- evaluate the startup's business model and suggest improvements; and
- guide the startup to polish and improve its pitch for investors and external viewers.

VP extends support to facilitate strategy, development of solutions, and trials of the products created by the startups accelerated by EDUGILD to make them revenue generating in due course. The following section describes the job description of EDUGILD's mentors and SMEs.

EDUGILD's Mentor Program

In our view, mentoring is a serious involvement that is focused on the worldview transformation and guidance of the individual mentee along with his/her startup approach. EDUGILD seeks mentors to help startups stay abreast of emerging business trends globally, cut down experimentation costs, and compress learning time. Mentors also provide support to hone skills related to collaboration, teamwork, negotiations, and networking.

In 20–24 week sessions, we facilitate participants to meet for 2–3 hours per month with mentors and SMEs, and more if the mentors and SMEs become intensely involved in helping make the business a success. The mentors can explore opportunities of early stage investment in the startups they are mentoring and in time, support them as VPs. The sessions that the mentors deliver involve a mix of group work, Q&A, and think–pair–share-led thought-provoking brainstorming. This has a reasonable alignment to what needs to be covered in the 16 weeks as a curriculum, and the milestones include developing a PMF, building the company infrastructure, and preparing for presentations to potential investors.

Hands-on mentoring from on-site experts followed by a regular virtual connect with mentors and SMEs is what ensures that there is adequate networking and a structured path to launch propositions within a finite run-up period. We also understand that mentors and SMEs of high caliber are extremely busy. In order to accommodate this, we offer a fine balance of structured/unstructured program slots at our accelerator. The startups also carefully analyze the mentors' and SMEs' profiles and expect them to do likewise in order to ensure that the mentors' time is optimally utilized to their benefit. The mentors'/SMEs' brief details are featured on the EDUGILD website and other marketing initiatives, so that the existing accelerating startups or those that wish to apply will get to know about the supreme quality of mentors that have agreed to join hands with EDUGILD for this cause.

In order to maximize the value of the mentor/SME's time devoted to EDUGILD, we ensure the following engagement parameters between them, EDUGILD, and the startups:

- *Aligning the mentor's specialties with mentoring needs:* Mentors and SMEs of high caliber have different skill sets and experiences. Our startups and we carry out thorough groundwork to ensure that they are invited to mentor the most strategically fit startup that will benefit from their presence and effectively utilize their time. Since timing is key here, the startups will need to connect with the mentor/SME (subject matter expert) during various phases of their journey, whether it is time to focus on consumer acquisition or raising money. In the long term, the intent will be for the startups to be encouraged to build one-on-one relations with the experts early on and utilize their time properly.

- *To the point every time:* EDUGILD keeps a close watch on the time when the experts are advising the startups, to ensure that they do not waste their time and get to the point with specific ask(s). It is our priority to ensure the startups know why exactly they need to reach the experts and what they are looking for—the "general guidance" trap will be eliminated from the mentor–startup engagement so that mutual trust is maintained at all times. Every engagement with the experts needs to have a time-bound, tangible, and impactful outcome so that the mentors and SMEs appreciate the connect, and their time is well spent.

- *Social and virtual media engagement:* We understand and respect the fact that physically being present at the venue of EDUGILD will not always work out and mentors/SMEs have their own priorities as well. Engaging with the experts online is encouraged, and, in our connected world, there are convenient tools and techniques to ensure that the mentees connect in a non-invasive and unintrusive manner. Getting the connect established in smarter ways is EDUGILD's commitment to show that we respect and care for the experts' time.

- *In-class sessions have serious stakes:* We have a structured program, components of which can be a lead to how the experts can plan their sessions. Mentor/SME sessions are like crash courses in all the elements of creating–running–developing a startup. This is a unique learning opportunity. The audience attending these sessions will have queries ready and will always be engaged and keen to soak in all the learning from the experts' experiences.

We also urge the mentors and SMEs to facilitate strengthening the EDUGILD ecosystem and spreading awareness amongst the edtech community. As a complimentary gesture, we arrange the following for the mentors/SMEs:

1. Travel and stay arrangements from their start point to EDUGILD and back.
2. Incidental charges on telecommunications and technology that they may incur when mentoring is done online/remotely.
3. Any support that our knowledge partner, MIT Group of Institutions, may be able to extend to them or their organization in terms of students, intellectual capital, projects, etc.
4. Honorarium for the hours they spend with our companies.

The success of our accelerator hinges on the mentoring done for startups in the fields of business management, technology,

finance, human capital development, product management, finance, operations, sales and marketing planning, and
GTM strategies. Since the new enterprises have management
teams that are usually very new to these domains, they fail
to understand the opportunities, pitfalls, and mitigation
techniques. This is where handholding and critical onsite/
offsite mentoring will make way for greater chances of their
success. The expert may choose to be a generic mentor or
an SME in specific domains and the timelines are mutually
worked out.

As of now, we have 18+ VPs and 100+ mentors. Each of
these partners is a strong contributor to the organizational
development of the companies. With a portfolio of 20+ startup
companies currently, the most obvious thing to do is to take
feedback from the existing employees. The companies I am
working with started off mostly as two-member teams, and
some of them now have close to 50 employees and are
growing. I encourage the startups to keep asking the existing
employees about what is working, what is not, and how to
make things better. This helps in the journey of a startup
toward being an organization. As an example, I know that
Simulanis' founder, Raman, is very passionate about his team.
Usually when we go out for a break/dinner, one or more of
his team members always accompany him. I like his spirit
of keeping a cohesive environment around. There will be a
day when he may not be able to take feedback one-on-one,
but then one can certainly conduct opinion polls.

As a startup begins to scale up, the leadership must refresh
its approach—a lot of delegation and management dilemmas

may come up. I may tell you that Ahhaa.com, which is a global entity now, does not have any full-time employees. The founders Daine and Ashwin have worked with freelancers, retainers, VPs, and mentors, and have still created a compelling proposition with a well-funded organization.

There was a time, and we winced about it, when Jay, the founder of ClassBoat, used to run ahead of time with a lot of next-level strategies. Many startup founders get into this leadership style where they seem to have conquered the present, and try to get to the future. They set out a broad vision. However, Jay did the right thing to listen to the people around, and, over the next three months, he focused on the depth of business rather than spreading it thin. So he scaled from ₹50,000 per month of revenue to 10 times this amount just by aligning the way the organization needed to focus on its priorities.

So, just to recapitulate, MuseIn lost its co-founder while the company was being incorporated. Today, the founder has become 10 times more confident because of the larger ecosystem that came his way. EDAPT by KnowHassles had to ease out one of their high-potential core team members, and managed it with no hard feelings. TrisLabs is doing great from a product development perspective, but they know we all are nervous about building a sales organization for them quickly. Amit (Vidya Robotics) is a show of strength and needs more people to delegate to. We realized of late that Abroad Shiksha has five technical resources and still the MVP has been delayed by six months. So we are getting into a resource-cost optimization discussion with them.

Initiatives such as those cited here, which balance founder directives with cross-functional interactions alongside the ecosystem, create a two-way dialog between the internal and external stakeholders. This can go a long way toward addressing organizational development and growth. If these companies hope to grow (no choice here) beyond being startups, they need to scale up with a refreshed leadership approach every time a new milestone is created, one that extracts the best from people instead of pushing them out early in the company's life cycle.

CHAPTER 7

Design Me to Life

The aim of UX as a subject matter is to study concepts, methods, and techniques of information architecture, usability engineering, information design, interaction design, visual design, ethnography, and prototype engineering, focusing on the aspects in which UX is essential. Historically, usability has covered aspects such as efficiency and learnability. Today, a large number of IT aspects include other measures of success such as playability, engagement, entertainment, immersion, and aesthetics. The UI/UX intervention program offered by MIT Institute of Design, Pune, trains learners to design and conduct usability studies of both the traditional aspects and those systems where experience is important.

I can quote a lot of companies in my portfolio who either benefitted through a great UI/UX intervention or are longing for one. According to the founders of ClassBoat, their biggest reorientation was in the UI/UX aspect of their product. Thereafter, it is business-critical to find the PMF before the bootstrapping cushion begins to run out. For the hundreds of startups I counsel each year, the first step is always to understand the problem they are solving—are they solving something that only the founders have faced or are they solving a real problem for which there will be paying customers. It is a textbook approach through which each startup working on an idea *has to* reach the PMF first. So, for this almost predictable process, is there a need to even consider the UI/ UX before the hypothesis of the solution is tested or will that be a waste of time? This is a generic question that has kept us at bay with regard to the UI/UX intervention for our companies. However, we have now started encouraging these interventions early enough because they shape the products from foundation to launch.

Product-Market Fit

[*Building something that is needed by someone willing to pay for it.*]

According to Ashwin, founder of Ahhaa.com, PMF means being in a universally expanding market with a solution that can satisfy the target audience's need and even bring to fore latent needs. For the founder of YoScholar, the PMF is about a multidisciplinary approach, where all the stakeholders in an ecosystem converge on one solution—in their case, it is the parents, schools, and suppliers/ vendors. So what is required is an evaluation of what a customer needs along with an equal emphasis on creating more customers and expanding the market. Every market that does not expand demonstrates cutthroat competition. An expanding market embraces competition and provides an opportunity for everyone to grow.

In order to check whether the product satisfies the market demand well, companies develop a MVP with only some core features. Such MVPs are then tested on early customers, which helps to build the final product. However, for ClassBoat, Simulanis, and StudyMarvel, the advisors not just scrapped their MVP but also sent them back to the drawing board to work on the PMF.

Hence, thinking and rethinking about what the customer can expect is a never-ending process.

Alongside creating a product, it is important to design something that can cross the chasm from *good to have* to *must have*. This is also how UI/UX intervention is perceived in the startup ecosystem, which until a few years ago was good to have and has become a must have now.

How Positive Is the Experience of the First User?

This is a hard question to answer. Nevertheless, no startup wants their early users to have a not-so-good experience. It is all about credibility, which has to be developed early enough. I have always stressed on the need for companies to have an effective UX solution, which can give wings to the product or service. It is the UX that defines how positive the actual user experience will be. And, the UX must be planned at the PMF level and then built into the MVP. As they say in the MasterChef kitchen, you taste the food with your eyes before you put it into your mouth. The UX concept for startup propositions is no different. The first impression is created on the customer by the overall experience, ease of navigation, and aesthetics, and not the product value proposition nor the stacks of technology behind it. *The first impression lasts forever* and sometimes you only have that one chance. Till date, YoScholar is desperate to figure out the appropriate UI/UX, as their business grows organically. However, they know that if the UI/UX is not taken care of, then success will be short-lived. If customers have a great first experience, they get hooked on as users and potential paying customers. If by any chance, they become early adopters, then the road is set for a great retention and acquisition story. A startup may create a great solution, but if it is difficult to experience what it does as well as how to use it, it generally goes beyond the attention span of the customer, making it difficult to sell.

As a part of my interactions with startups, we have three partners who contribute to UI/UX design analysis. One of them is our own in-house institute called MIT Institute of Design (MITID)—one of the best design institutes in the country. Their team has always been supportive with the initial UI/UX advisory for our companies. We also have a strategic tie-up with copods.co. These two organizations have very sincere UI/UX minds and work closely to advise our companies on their strategies. One more thing that needs to be remembered is that customers do not have all the time to keep giving you a chance. If their first experience is not up to the mark, they will not care about the product proposition. They will not even care to give it a chance thereafter, no matter how much you follow them up for it.

The User Interface

The users interact with your product through the UI. The UI is what meets the users' eyes when they begin to experience your proposition. The more appealing and easy to use it is, the more the stickiness of the user. UI mistakes are painful to rectify. When I first met the founders of Abroad Shiksha, they exuberated passion and energy. However, their UI/UX was a far cry from what we wanted the users to perceive about them. In the last one year, they have come a long way to enhance their UI. However, we remember it causing us to lose a lot of valuable time. Almost 20–30 percent of their potential users are now coming from online channels and this is just the beginning.

One of the best UI/UX brand identity realignments was done by Gradopedia, now AmbitionUp. The spotlight feature describes the challenges faced by the company and the need to change the experience quotients (in the founder's own words).

SPOTLIGHT: Gradopedia Is now AmbitionUp—Here's to the Transition!

We broke through to EDUGILD in early 2016—opening doors to the best launchpad any company could get in our space.

At the end of the accelerator program, we did pilots, worked out a tangible offering, built an MVP in ₹50,000 (which did work end-to-end), and then decided to invest our time and effort into the product.

Today, as we push for the beta launch, we're taking a step toward something that has been a year in the making.

A bigger brand, a bigger vision and a bolder approach.

AmbitionUp

What Was Wrong with Our Current Brand?

We conceived of Gradopedia when I was still in college; we started as a one-page website that would allow final-year graduates like me to understand which career to pick and which one would match their personalities and interests.

Attempting to be the Wikipedia for graduates, we did our share of research to curate as many as 20 careers across various segments. While Gradopedia meant different things to different people, it was not what we were intending to build. These were the views various segments had about the services offered:

- HR personnel—A platform only for fresh graduates?
- Graduates—A platform to learn something online?
- Placement cells—A platform that could help one prepare for interviews?

Hence, we would spend more time trying to explain what we did rather than in doing what we could. And in all fairness, the old logo did not help!

So, What's with the New Identity?
Throughout our interactions with people and the process of explaining the concept, we realized one thing that we were not going to stop at freshers. Visualize a scenario where the average graduate could get a dream job, a settled graduate could improve himself, and an improved graduate could feel further uplifted. So just like the graduates we love and ourselves, we would not settle, simply because *we love the pursuit, the chase, and the feeling of following your ambition, however crazy or unrealistic it may seem.* Thus presenting, AmbitionUp.

Under the new brand, our core focus is toward building career paths, and we strongly believe the following:

1. Our graduates are extremely talented; all they are missing is someone to direct them in the right direction and provide personalized advice.

2. Employability is poorly defined; you cannot ask aptitude-related questions and judge someone for any career. Emerging careers require specialized skills, so employability is different for each of them.

3. Graduates can be given the right perspective and context in a career, and that alone can lead to a more aware and skilled workforce.

With this in mind, we are taking a big step toward ensuring a personalized career path for all. So here's to an even more enriching journey forward. AmbitionUp helps

- aspirants to explore careers and get to know how employable they are, apply for jobs, or get guidance on tangible improvement steps and
- employers to post jobs and restrict applications to only those aspirants who meet all their education, experience, personality, and skill requirements.

Let us now move on to the UX challenges of Edorble. Edorble helps teachers and students create, publish, and use social, 3D worlds. They also make custom 3D/VR apps for learning and/or training. As a company, they listed the following areas of enhancement (the core elements of their UI):

- *Audience.*
  - A teacher who may have experimented unsuccessfully or was too intimidated by current online tools but is researching for ways to get his/her class online synchronously.
- *Proposal.*
  - We are making online learning personal, playful, and painless.

- ○ *Reasoning*—It addresses the fact that we try to remove friction, something these teachers have possibly experienced before. Its mention there is more than that, as it adds playful notes. Moreover, it is in person, which reflects almost real-time, synchronous learning.

- *Call to action (introduction).*

  - ○ Want to bring the magic of the physical classroom online? We're looking for 1,000 pioneers.
  - ○ *Reasoning*—It is more than overcoming challenges. It also addresses the fact that we're trying to create the same experience as in the physical classroom.

- *Call to action.*

  - ○ Apply now (we need some commitment)
  - ○ Reasoning

- *Missing.*

  - ○ Next level of teaching through tech; we're here to disrupt

These elements are reflected to a certain extent on their website [www.edorble.com], and they wanted to learn how they could improve on that front. Post improvements, Edorble now has one of the most friendly UI/UXs. The new UI is shown here:

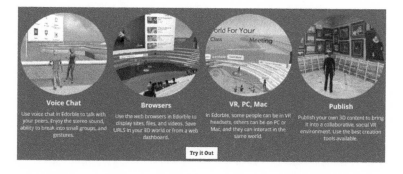

Voice Chat — Use voice chat in Edorble to talk with your peers. Enjoy the stereo sound, ability to break into small groups, and gestures.

Browsers — Use the web browsers in Edorble to display sites, files, and videos. Save URLS in your 3D world or from a web dashboard.

VR, PC, Mac — In Edorble, some people can be in VR headsets, others can be on PC or Mac, and they can interact in the same world.

Publish — Publish your own 3D content to bring it into a collaborative, social VR environment. Use the best creation tools available.

Try it Out

Another case in point is Simulanis.com, a successful AR/VR learning development company. Their UI/UX transition has been slow due to too many opportunities at hand.

The Simulanis UI/UX is now seamless and competes with world-class companies in the same space. Simulanis is a multi-award winning edtech company leveraging AR, VR, and 3D simulation technologies to develop cutting-edge interactive, engaging, and immersive products for the education, learning, and skill domains.

Their products cut across a range of industrial and education sectors, while addressing some of the most pressing skill and learning challenges. Laced with the highest degree of interactivity and backed by proprietary assessment-driven and trademarked "SCISSOR" methodology, their products enable customers to retentively learn some of the most difficult concepts with ease. With a strong focus on continuous innovation, their multitalented in-house team of "rockstar" designers, artists, developers, and engineers work tirelessly to bring about a revolutionary transformation and/or disruption in their sector of operation.

A UI/UX should give one the feeling of meeting someone through their digital identity. Hence, compassion and empathy should be embedded in the way the interface and experience are designed. UI/UX issues can lead people to uninstall certain apps from their devices due to dissatisfaction and we definitely would not want that for our companies. The lesson learnt is that it is very easy to develop the front end and back end of an app or a website. However, it is incredibly difficult to create an interface that is inviting, visually appealing, and compelling to use.

Designing for Enterprise as Opposed to Consumer Products: Is It Different?

Our UI/UX partner company copods.co has a fair view on the UI/UX strategies for products in the enterprise and consumer space, as explained by Anish, the founder.

Over the last few years, the distinction between designing experiences for enterprise products versus consumer products has significantly narrowed and is undistinguishable in a few scenarios, thanks to the fast evolving and adopted trend for "consumerization of enterprise products," and the change in user behavioral patterns as well as expectations.

Today, enterprise users are exposed to a wide array of consumer products as well as social applications in their day-to-day life at work and home. Flexible enterprise policies such as "bring your own device" (BYOD) and "choose your own tool" (CYOT) have exposed employees to common productivity/communication tools in their work life and have proven to enhance employee productivity. Growing collaboration and accessibility needs (from anywhere and anytime) owing to the change in business dynamics as well as user behavior have forced enterprise product creators to rethink their strategies (e.g., Microsoft Office versus Google Docs) and reorient themselves to adapt to social platforms and related features. The overlapping experiences have uncovered an open design canvas for us, *the experience designers*, and there is a noticeable change in the design thought and approach. Mobile, gaming, etc., design paradigms have become a stimulus, and seem to be widely embraced for shaping intuitive and personalized enterprise product experiences.

UI standardization between consumer and enterprise products is imminent and I believe that design paradigms, if embraced responsibly and judiciously, can significantly improve product adoption, engagement, and user efficacy.

Through my collaboration with several Fortune 500 companies as well as startups serving enterprise and consumer needs, several interesting lessons have been learnt, and I believe there are various challenges that still face us in enterprise product designing. The following are a few aspects that may be worth keeping in mind while strategizing toward solutions.

**Design Innovation Is Important and Equally Risky
If Not Considered Judiciously**

As designers we enjoy shaping new design patterns, offer newness to each and every product experience we engage with, and thereby always push boundaries for creating a difference. Yearning for design innovation at every opportunity may at times result in expensive outcomes. Enterprise products usually have significant legacy in terms of front-end/back-end technologies, in-house features, and functionality that have matured with time. They are backed by notable customer loyalty and a sizeable end-user base that may have fallen prey to "learnt helplessness". The dynamics places the designers in a tricky situation, as weaving radical and rapid innovation into the conventional and learnt interaction patterns may work to the detriment of the product's usability and overall user acceptance, and bloat support costs.

Over the last few years, I have got several opportunities to help design UX for enterprise products in the cloud computing, data center, networking, enterprise security, insurance and banking, employee productivity, healthcare, and law and litigation domains. I have realized that no matter how innovative an experience a designer creates, certain conventional interaction design paradigms have become an established and comfortable industry norm, which are easily accepted by enterprise product companies and well understood by their customers and the end-users of the product. This could be owing to the fact that many established enterprise products are progressively migrating to web/thin client and mobile versions. This situation many-at-times brews frustration and is considered a creativity dampener.

Having said this, based on my experience, I would say that it is better to accept the norm and invest our energies and creativities in other areas of the product experience such as the overall information architecture, user journeys, micro-interactions, messaging, and contextual help, which could create a significant difference in the overall product experience. Offering playful and radically new interaction paradigms such as collapsed drawer/hamburger menus (which may hide primary gateways under a click), creative iconography-based slide-in/out menus (which may become hard to relate with and thus hamper discoverability), cards as a primary alternative to data-grids (which may hamper the data consumption scale), etc., are received as being "good looking" and "cool" by product and marketing teams; however, these may be perceived as being counter-intuitive and inefficient during design validation studies with prospective/actual users and resisted by engineering teams, and are thus a futile effort.

A change from customary practices often induces significant unlearning and learning, and may result in being detrimental to overall end-user productivity. As designers, we need to be sensitive to the enterprise product ecology and acquaint ourselves with the "when?" and "where?" to decide whether to adopt conventional or innovative paradigms, thereby keeping existing users happy as well as lowering the barrier for new ones.

A "T-shaped" Profile Is Essential

In a T-shaped profile, the horizontal line reflects the width of expertise and the vertical line represents the depth of expertise. Such profiles are needed in design-led profiles. Being a designer for a consumer product of which you may be or are a user such as Facebook, WhatsApp, etc., will be easier to connect with and design for as opposed to designing experiences for unknown enterprise products. Designing for specialized user profile(s) situated in unique environmental setups requires sound domain technology and contextual understanding. For acquiring complete understanding of the product ecosystem and experiencing what end-users experience, the designer should have the knack and motivation for conducting research studies with stakeholders as well as end-users. As a result, for designing successful enterprise products, being a competent designer may not be enough, as the "experience designer" will need to have the qualities of a researcher, a good understanding of front-end UI development technologies and their influence on design, and good analytical skills.

Success Criteria Are Identical and Have a Long Lifespan

Shaping a consumer product offers the designer quick gratification in terms of public visibility and acknowledgment from thousands of users and hence is usually a sought-after task. As designers, we often distinguish between business and end-user goals, try and identify commonalities, and create a design strategy that will cater to both needs. In the case of consumer products, it so happens that the originally conceived product's UI design experience often gets skewed and diluted with time owing to the disparity between business and user goals, resulting in conflicting opinions. For example, a multimedia product company may focus on monetization via ads and hence maneuver the user's experience in a manner that may lead them to traverse through as many ads as possible before accessing the audio/video content, or intrude by splashing ads while the user is viewing the content. An end-user's goal, on the other hand, will be to view a video of interest as quickly as possible without interference.

An enterprise product development life cycle could be long and challenging, and it may take more than a year or two for the complete product to see the light of day. Having said that, the best part about designing an enterprise product experience is that the business and end-user goals for the majority are identical and remain meaningful for a long time. For example, employee productivity is directly proportional to enterprise savings/revenue. Hence, one would be designing for a common vision with a lasting impact.

For a consumer product, short cycles of updates are imperative for survival, while in the case of enterprise product design, longevity is the key to success. As a result, it is extremely important to identify the business as well as end-user success criteria for an enterprise product carefully and shape design paradigms with the characteristics of scalability and futurism.

End-User Profile as Oppose to Personas

We generally use the word "profile" and "persona" interchangeably even though their meaning and relevance are different. *User personas*—the more commonly used jargon—are descriptive in nature and a semi-fictional representation of an ideal product user. Personas work well when the unknowns are greater and the product has to be designed based on assumed facts about the probable target groups. User profiles are prescriptive, as they are outlined based on facts and known user data. Enterprise product users are known, and hence outlining a user profile is more relevant in this context, as data for each aspect about the specific user will be readily available with the enterprise. In a recent project engagement, we went to the extent of talking with HR representatives for actual job descriptions of targeted user profiles. Subsequently, we also connected with the actual users for contextual understanding and ratification. The exercise gave us a deep understanding of the end users' psyche, goals, and motivations, and uncovered a few extremely insightful a-day-in-the-life-of nuances, which otherwise could have been overlooked, resulting in skewed outcomes.

Design Paradigms with a Futuristic Character

Enterprises could have a world-class looking web product, a friendly mobile application, and an awesome CRM system. However, if you were to ask them if their int./ext. product ecosystems are connected, the answers would usually be "no," "not required," "not yet," "hopefully soon," "that's why we are talking to you," and so on. As designers, we invest a lot of our time and energy in acquiring a holistic perspective of the product ecosystem during the very early stages of project engagement, and, in the case of a legacy enterprise product, you would often have made suggestions such as "shaping an omni-channel experience will increase user productivity and save operational costs," "a responsive, adaptive, or hybrid experience may be more suitable from a futuristic product adoption/usage perspective based on foreseen changes in user behavioral patterns," etc. While the stakeholders appreciate all suggestions and personally love to pursue the ideal path, more often than not, the design scope usually gets curtailed by a myopic need owing to budgetary and time-to-release constraints. This leads to adopting a blinkered and tactical approach for shaping the product UX design. Moreover, the race against time often steers designers toward cutting corners for faster outcomes.

Lessons from past project experiences have made me believe that, as designers, we should always design futuristic paradigms despite the immediate/near-term needs, thus mitigating the impending risks. If we adopt the basic design fundamentals for adaptive/responsive grid structures, atomic and modular design components, fluid layouts, as well as scalable graphic and font libraries, the product design foundation will be robust and capable of absorbing future needs. There may be a deviation from the originally planned effort/time, but the quality of the outcomes will be worth every penny invested.

Primarily Mouse/Keyboard Driven Behavior

The advent of touch-enabled interfaces has significantly influenced the design language of products (e.g., large tappable areas/objects, gesture-driven interactions). Owing to the common trend of current digital interactions, we tend to ignore the usage of the mouse and keyboard as an integral input device for enterprise applications, thereby leading to overlooked behaviors, less than optimum layouts for immediate to near-term needs, etc. This often leads to cycles of negotiation with the product owners and engineers, and skewed outcomes. While, there is nothing wrong in designing for the future, as experience designers, it is critical to ensure that our decisions do not compromise the immediate and short-term goals. In a past project, we mitigated a similar situation by introducing viewing modes (similar to Gmail's "Comfortable, Cosy, and Compact" display densities) and adopted adaptive design constructs for fluidity and scale. In doing so, we easily accommodated immediate, short-term, and long-term goals from the business as well as users' perspective and offered a higher level of control.

Accessibility

Have you ever experienced customers complaining about the interface colors being washed out and not appealing at their end? Our fondness for Apple Mac machines is the cause. As designers, we diligently conduct all color anomaly tests in our systems before delivering to our customers and often tend to forget that the customer/end user machines in the enterprise world are mostly Windows-based PCs/laptops. Try viewing your visual designs on a standard Windows-based PC, and you will realize why your customers are straining their vocal cords. As a process, it is important that you test your visual designs across different machines and displays including standard Windows-based PCs and laptops. The traditional test for color contrast wherein one takes a B/W printout of the designs works well too.

Intensive Training and Specialists for Customization Is Passé

How many times have you really needed to scan help files or seek long hours of assistance while interacting with a consumer product? Generally your answer will be none or insignificant. In a situation wherein the assistance required is high, the product adoption curve is extremely low and a high drop-off rate is experienced. In today's day and age, customers and end users expect a similar experience while interacting with enterprise products. Customers of your product would not like to create a heavy dependence on their vendors for the smooth functioning of their enterprise applications and business. While end-users would like an experience that aligns with their innate behavior, reliable training as well as support channels for everyday work-life needs is considered a barrier.

A well-designed people experience impact (PEI) approach exploring the relationship between people (potential customers + customers) and brands, and how the interactions with different brand service channels influence the entire journey from being potential customers to loyal customers, could reveal the secret recipe for retaining customers and engaging potential ones.

CHAPTER 8

Feed Self, Then Get Fed: Business Development and Revenue Generation

Revenue generation is a habit and must supersede the urge to become a magnet for funds. When companies approach me, I make the ground rules clear: Work with us to become revenue-ready and not fund-needy. There is a possibility that many companies would not understand what I mean. However, the companies in my portfolio know very well what it implies.

The importance of revenue is back in discussion after a few years of hyper-availability of funds. While the credibility of the founders, MVP, and so on, may be leading indicators of a company's future, the early and steady enhancement of revenue is a lagging indicator of companies poised for greater heights. So in my network, we have three types of companies: ones that are scaling up with revenue steadily, others that are in early revenue stage, and finally those which are launching their product/s. We do not have any examples of companies only pushing for funding and waiting for that to happen until the next steps forward are taken. Once the companies have gone through six months of structured acceleration process, I insist on working with the founders on something loosely termed as *enhanced acceleration*. This focuses primarily on business enhancement, PR, and technology stability. It is for this reason that a couple of companies I am working with have reached the break-even point in 18 months of our professional relationship. So either they attract funding due to their performance or the need to get funded reduces substantially. The taste of revenue is sweet and it takes away any bitterness of sleepless nights.

It is also a fact that investors value revenue projections more than words. However, in early discussions, revenue projections are meaningless. Hence, every company in the network that has met an investor has done so only after the revenues have started trickling in. This is when their numbers are realistic and actual, and not mere projections. This leads the ecosystem, including PR, to perceive the startups positively.

Finally, the lesson learnt is that every founder has to *sell, sell, and sell*. One cannot sit back and say, "I don't have it in me"; this is not an option. One must sell; if there is no revenue, there is no company. I will explain this in the following sections by illustrating the experiences I have had with the startups I am engaged with.

ClassBoat

As a case in point, ClassBoat has been business accelerated from a revenue of ₹50,000 per month to ₹5 lakhs per month. They have a burn rate of ₹3.5 lakh per month. So, since September 2017, they have been revenue positive. They moved from spending 80 percent of their time in raising funds to spending 90 percent of their time in enhancing their revenue. This led to a course correction in the business model and the sales teams being strengthened. The top 20 customer accounts are now directly managed by the founders.

Pune-based ClassBoat, a marketplace of course providers and individual instructors, was established in 2016 when husband–wife duo Chaitanya Salgarkar and Renu Salgarkar wanted to join hobby classes but were unaware of any trusted source through which they could find good instructors. Almost for 14 years, the founders had been working abroad. When they returned to India, they wanted to join classes themselves and found that the market in India is very unorganized. There are a lot of options, but people do not know which is a good one to go for. The startup currently lists more than 250 activities across areas such as dance, art, film, sports, and technology.

ClassBoat helps large-scale course providers fill empty seats. Users can get free trials and then book sessions at discounted prices. They generate around 7,000–8,000 leads every month for which they already have paying customers, to whom they sell these curated leads. So they understand what course providers need and get them curated leads with the most chances of successful conversion. The startup generates revenue on a lead-based model, wherein the instructors pay the platform depending on the number of potential customers they gain out of it. ClassBoat, which has already raised money from a few angel investors and EDUGILD, may be raising its Series A round. They are now in a revenue-positive situation and hence are exploring expanding to Delhi, Bengaluru, Mumbai, and Ahmedabad.

ClassBoat provides real-life testimonials as evidence. Sapna Hosmath, a corporate behavioral skills trainer, moved to Pune from Bengaluru in June. She wanted to enroll her five-year-old son to a keyboard class, but had no idea who to approach. While she was browsing through the Internet, Hosmath came across ClassBoat's website, where she found a keyboard teacher for her son as well as a guitar instructor for herself!

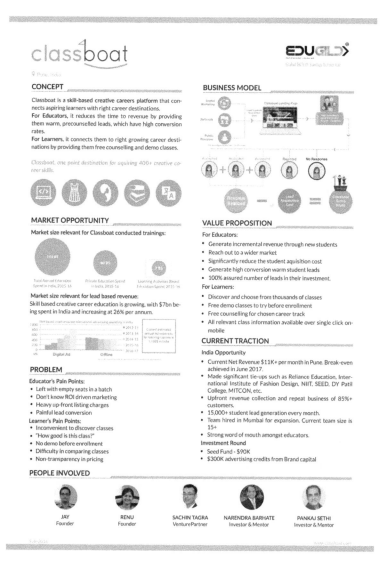

YoScholar.com

Let us look at our second scaling up company, YoScholar.com. Their gross merchandize value in 2016 was close to ₹1 crore, and we joined hands with a mandate of pushing the revenue to the next level. In the calendar year 2017, they achieved a GMV in excess of ₹5 crore, all because of a planned division of responsibilities. One of the founders focuses on revenue and the other keeps him shielded from all operational and ecosystem pressures—an amazing journey in the making.

An important lesson learnt on enhancing revenue was through the rebranding of SchoolSaamaan to YoScholar. The viable difference was that under the earlier brand, the company could not augment its offering, and hence was facing early revenue saturation. SchoolSaamaan.com was launched in Bengaluru in March 2015 as an e-commerce marketplace to provide need-based educational products such as uniforms, books, shoes, etc., online, with an evolving focus on students at the center of its strategy. Over the last 1.5 years, it has expanded its reach to four cities (Bengaluru, NCR, Hyderabad, and Pune) with products listed for over 250+ schools and deliveries across India. During this time, it has also broadened its offering from need-based products to nice to have products (such as accessories, fancy dresses, educational and sports kits among others, educational toys). Today it has 60+ sellers catering to a large number of students and their parents. With its new brand (YoScholar), it reaffirms its commitment to be a facilitator for students, providing them with everything they need through their entire duration of learning and development.

YoScholar represents and highlights the founders' focus on keeping the student at the center of the education ecosystem and ensuring that their actions are aligned toward the interests of students. This branding change also highlights the broadening of their line of products and services to out-of-school needs, which students require for their overall growth. The change also underlines the plan to include non-product offerings (services) such as various interest and hobby classes for their customers. As of now, YoScholar has 10+ service partners who offer their education services through the YoScholar portal. All in all, this realignment has improved their GMV from ₹1 crore to ₹5 crores year-on-year.

EDU GILD

CONCEPT

YoScholar, an Edyoo Technologies product, is an education commerce platform providing tangible value to the stakeholders across the education ecosystem:

* **Parents / Students:** Single marketplace for all learning, education and development needs of a child in and out of the classroom
* **Sellers / Vendors:** Closely working with sellers/vendors of education products for enhanced reach & operational efficiency. We are building seller side solutions to manage offline/online orders, payments & fulfilments.
* **Service Providers (co-curricular/extra-curricular activities):** Solution to manage their classes, batches, subscriptions, payments and communication.
* **Institutes:** Our products assist institutes by offering convenient, transparent and reliable virtual stores for parents while ensuring complete transparency and control for institutes.

MARKET OPPORTUNITY

The Indian education market itself is > $ 100 billion and is expected to grow fast and far. Its key addressable components are:

* Uniform & School Supplies – $11bn.
* Online Education, Coaching & Counselling – $6.6bn.
* Summer Camp & Activities – $734mn.

Further, the target customers of above market closely overlap with the Books & Toys industries.

PROBLEM

With time becoming precious every passing day, parents still spend considerable time & efforts in identifying, locating and procuring the most basic products and services needed for their children rather than investing this time with them.

Further, technology is rapidly changing the way education is conceived and consumed, and so are the priorities related to development and learning. This is creating tremendous opportunity for Edtech companies to make a difference.

However, on the flipside, the student/parent is left struggling to identify what's best and often the decision is made in favor of the loudest or the cheapest.

SOLUTION

In the ever-changing education marketplace, we are positioning as the trusted constant for parents & students to navigate & identify what's best suited for them.

* Unified platform for Institute authorized merchandize
* Best in class Edtech products to connect end users with innovative solutions.
* User verified, trust-based products and services.
* End to end information related to education, development & learning.

BUSINESS MODEL

Market Place
* Hosting need-based products (Uniforms & Text Books), costumes, EdTech products and services - Online coaching, counselling, sports coaching, etc.

Technology Solutions
* Vendors entrenched in Institute's ecosystem - Vendor apps, marketplace, analytics & fulfilment to scale their operations.
* Institutions - Exclusive virtual store to manage all transactions.
* Edtech Companies - Plug and play market place providing access to a tech savvy user base across India.

VALUE PROPOSITION

Parents/Students: Unified & trusted platform to meet all the education & development related requirement.
Institutions: Online management of products & services facilitating education.
Vendors: A pan India user base, technology solutions and analytics & scale.

CURRENT TRACTION

* Authorized merchandise of 300+ Institutions and 85+ Vendors.
* 13 K transactions and $750K Sales in Jan - Apr 2018.
* Expected sales of $4mn in FY19

PEOPLE INVOLVED

AMIT MISHRA
Co-Founder

CHHAVI MISHRA
Co-Founder

KAPIL ARORA
CTO

SACHIN TORNE
Venture Partner

StudyMarvel

StudyMarvel is our youngest prodigy. They are young of years but very wise—a great team and brilliant VPs. They have a unique model for generating early revenue along with pushing the MVP ahead. So, it is amazing to see these young enthusiasts generating revenue through consultancy and investing the funds into the AR product.

STUDY █ MARVEL

CONCEPT

Studymarvel is an Augmented Reality Platform for K-12 segment and Book Publishers which lets the user Explore. Visualize and Save digital media like 3D models, images, videos, hyperlinks and more in the physical space, and superimpose storyboards and lessons practically anywhere on any object.

With a simple scan, students can access thousands of 3D models representing anything from a part of the human anatomy to a famous monument to a structure of an atom.

MARKET OPPORTUNITY

- Augmented Reality market is expected to be worth $56.8 bn by 2020 with a CAGR of 132%.
- The United States, Europe, and India are the three leading markets which are actively adopting AR and we have 200M+ AR users worldwide.
- Use of education apps by students has grown by over 217% YoY. The average time spent by students on mobile devices has grown by over 91%.
- Students from classes 6 to 12 spent 32% more time studying online.

PROBLEM

The traditional lecture is still one of the most common teaching methods since it has the advantage of being able to reach many students in one economical time slot.
This approach, of course, rarely allows for the sort of interaction and active learning that more hands-on, practical sessions (such as lab work or tutorials) can facilitate.
This leads to the less interaction of the student with the subject, and they remember only 40% of what they learned in school. Learning Pyramid also states that retention rate can be increased up to 75% if you practice it by doing it.
More often than not, schools do not have enough resources to equip students with hands-on subject-specific equipment and experiments. Further, these learning materials get worn down, lose their relevance, and get misplaced over time.

SOLUTION

Explore and Augment 3D models from the StudyMarvel 3D Library and AR Education Packs with pre-defined 3D Models. Students can enhance a physical book with AR properties, like pop-out figures, optional links to extra information, word definitions or even take notes anywhere and everywhere.

By viewing augmented models, the students can gain a better understanding of the concepts they are studying by having an immersive experience every time. Prototypes, physical models, illustrations, and posters can be replaced by placing 3D models in physical arena.

BUSINESS MODEL

Freemium Subscription Plan : Students can access 3D models from a wide range of library and create their own markers.

Platform as a Subscription Model : Lets the Publisher Augment their books and provide immersive learning.

Professional : Custom 3D models with enhances interaction, shading and colors, meshing, show videos, link, pictures on Books with own assets.

VALUE PROPOSITION

Eye-Catching Presentations :
By making learning as engaging as gaming, we are awakening curiosity in students around the world.

Portable And Less Expensive Learning Materials :
Prototypes, physical models, and detailed illustrations and posters are all extremely expensive.

Higher Retention :
With a simple scan, students can access augmented models representing anything from a part of the human anatomy to a famous monument to a structure of an atom.

CURRENT TRACTION

- Launched Alpha Version in August 2017
- Onboarded 'Learn By Fun', Central India's largest K-12 Publisher, to launch more than 800 AR experiences for K-8 having a reach of more than 2000 schools in India.

PEOPLE INVOLVED

YASH BODANE
Cofounder and CEO

MAYANK LAMBHATE
Product Head | Chief Architect

MANISH UPADHYAY
Venture Partner

ATINDRIYA BOSE
Venture Partner

KidsTriangle

KidsTriangle is a company with the founders working from Boston and India. Their VP, Dr Harish, has made them a revenue-generating company in no time. With 17 schools and 850 parents onboard and 500+ parents logging in everyday, their monthly subscription charge is INR 40–50 per child and their present monthly revenue is ₹40,000. It is pure revenue play and each of our ecosystem partners keeps this aspect on top priority.

ChangeMyPath

Online education is currently stuck in a "video-and-a-quiz" format that is ineffective and uninspiring. High-quality interactive content is more engaging and more effective, but is also very expensive and difficult to update after deployment. ChangeMyPath is taking online education and job skills training to the next dimension by providing easy-to-use tools for creating rich and exciting 3D games and simulations as part of training content. Their founder Zack was in India recently with only two objectives: to find an Indian business head and start a dialogue to be able to generate revenue in India.

CONCEPT

- Automate the School's education, teaching and administration to reduce human dependency.
- Consolidate Schools IT vendors into one provider to make education System affordable & sustainable.
- Full automatic ecosystem (Parents, teacher, home) integration helps to drive true personalized education for students.

MARKET OPPORTUNITY

$20bn Preschools and Schools industry in India with a CAGR 30% YOY.

PROBLEM

- Too many School's IT vendors solution leads to system defragmentation and hence increasing expense and management headache.
- Technology needs human input to drive & innovate it, Human are lazy by definition, and hence, most of the edtech solutions turn out to be less useful, and more expensive.
- Personalized education never took off due to too much manual data entry and lack of full ecosystem integration (Student's health, family, school).

SOLUTION

- Become single vendor IT solution provider for Schools (ERP, Mobile app, CCTV, GPS, Digital marketing, Admission leads provider etc.).
- Automate edtech technology using AI to remove human dependency and bring huge affordability & faster adoption.
- Integrate minimum required ecosystem (Child's health, family, school) to deliver true personalized education.

BUSINESS MODEL

- Primary Customer (Preschools) pays for yearly subscription of services.
- Primary Customer data (preschool children) gets fed to Secondary Customer (Schools) as paid admission leads.

VALUE PROPOSITION

- Significant cost saving of 5x; to get all the services from a single vendor.
- All services are fully automated and require no manual work; to reduce man power salary from schools.
- Fully Automated result driven integrated Digital Marketing for schools/preschools.
- Largely automated End to End School IT solution provider (Mobile app, CCTV, GPS, Website, etc.).
- Fully Auto personalized Preschool education using advanced AI Solution to boost early childhood development.

CURRENT TRACTION

- 100+ Paying customers (Preschools, Schools) across Delhi, Mumbai, Noida, Haryana, Rajasthan.
- Early Revenue $27K per Year.

PEOPLE INVOLVED

AMIT KUMAR
Co-Founder

WILBERT MACCLAY
Co-Founder

LALIT KUMAR
Co-Founder

VIKAS YADAV
Co-Founder

HARISH CHAUDHRY
Venture Partner

Change My Path

CONCEPT

ChangeMyPath is transforming job skills training. It is building a system of customizable 3D simulations (for use on computers, mobile devices, and AR / VR wearables). This will offer companies a platform to deliver interactive job skills training content in a much more engaging way than the conventional e-Learning courses.

MARKET OPPORTUNITY

ChangeMyPath's product has similar applications in higher education allowing for future horizontal expansion into this market. The e-Learning market is worth $49.9B, with $8.7B now attributed to mobile devices, and growing rapidly. Change My Path also expands its reach by branching into AR/VR wearable devices.

PROBLEM

Currently, if a company wants interactive training content, it can cost more than $250K and it costs extra time and money for any updates. This makes it almost impossible to create content and/or keep it consistent with their products or procedures.

SOLUTION

Using the Company's authoring system, customers create the employee training content, map the course components onto one of the Company's game modules, and the employees are then able to access the interactive material via web browser or mobile device, anytime and anywhere. The result is a more engaging experience, improved information retention, and better trained employees.

The company's customers already include a large multi-billion dollar company with 9,000 employees and more are in beta-trials. The company's modules have the capability to expand to AR/VR wearable devices, creating simulated 3D environments for training and also delivery via Facebook Messenger app.

BUSINESS MODEL

The company's revenue channels revolve around licensing fees, and are easily scalable at minimal cost. License fees for using the Change My Path framework to deliver a customer's training content will be tiered by number of employees, license fees for delivering existing training content will be charged at a flat percentage, and independent developers can also create content and sell through the company for a license fee.

VALUE PROPOSITION

- Interactive job skills training.
- More engagement than conventional E-learning classes.
- Improved information retention.
- Better trained employees.
- Creating simulated 3D environments for training and delivering by Facebook Messenger app.

CURRENT TRACTION

Launching with First Customer

First customer is a large, multi-billion dollar company with 9,000 employees, focused on fire and safety equipment. Customer will be using Change My Path's software to train its new employees.

Roll Out to Additional Customers

The next set of early adopter customers have been lined up to begin a roll out of the product. Several of these customers are large multinational companies.

India Opportunity

- Engagement initiated with potential partners
- In process to hire India head.

PEOPLE INVOLVED

| ZACK KARLSSON | DAVID MANDEL | STEPHEN WILLIAMS | DR. KEITH DEVLIN | MARTY BRODBECK | SACHIN TAGRA |
| Founder | Chairman | CTO | Board Member | Board Member | Venture Partner |

Ahhaa.com

Ahhaa.com is a company founded by a monk of 17 years and a mother of two, who became entrepreneurs early in their lives. The company was pivoted at EDUGILD to be a technology player rather than a personal one-on-one sessions provider. Today they boast of revenues from Sony Music, Saavn, Jio App, Cambridge University Press, and Avantika University (MP). Their business partner Karan Grover has ensured that the founders' eyes are set to be a unicorn (billion-dollar startup) in the space of solutions for mind, body, and soul. The founder is an ex-mentor of the legendary Michael Jackson, and now the company collaborates with Grammy Award Winner A. R. Rahman, who invests in it. The company's culture is driven by *revenue at the core with austerity*.

Consider the dimensional change that the founders of Ahhaa.com went through when being aligned toward revenue with a cause. When the former monk, with strong connections in the music world, and a former corporate executive got together, the resulting venture was unique.

Ashwin Srisailam, a former monk turned entrepreneur, who has hung out with Michael Jackson and counts A. R. Rahman among his friends, and Diane Bacchus-Quddus got together to set up Ahhaa.com in 2015. Their app, launched by A. R. Rahman, was then a platform for inner growth and fulfilment. After being selected for acceleration at EDUGILD in 2016, it has undergone a change in what it is doing. The focus has now shifted to creating "Ahhaa spaces" or meditation zones in corporate and educational campuses as well as making a version of the app available to millions of users.

According to Diane and Ashwin,

The aim is to help with inner growth, using content for inner well-being. The first such space is up at the Cambridge University Press premises in New Delhi. This is a light design lab geared towards immersive content using virtual reality. While the content has been created based on insights from us (the founders), the music for the Ahhaa space has been specially licensed by A. R. Rahman himself. The content focuses on four key areas—insights, inspiration, music, and meditation.

The trigger for setting up this venture was the realization that most people in corporate jobs and students face a high degree of stress in their daily lives, which impacts both their personal and professional lives. These spaces use virtual reality—audio and video content presented in small three-five minute capsules—on specific topics, aimed toward inner growth and "feeling awesome."

The plan is to expand this over time to other educational institutes as well as collaborate with other people, including celebrities, to create content. According to the founders, the world has 3.2 billion workers, and the expected market opportunity is pegged at $320 billion and growing at a rate of 12.2 percent, if one is to consider an average spend of $100. If 50 percent of the market is considered as available for Ahhaa's solutions, then there is a potential to address $160 billion market. Ahhaa aspires to able to target 10 percent of this market and hence, has a captive market opportunity of $16 billion annually. Sony Music, Saavn, and Jio app have launched Ahhaa solutions now, generating revenue for the company.

CONCEPT

Launched by Oscar & Grammy award winner A.R. Rahman, Ahhaa is a platform that focuses on inner growth & self -development like never before. It is co-created by a former monk of 17 years & a Mom with a background of Corporate America to deliver unique mind education. It helps people deal with daily life challenges leading to personal & professional growth & happiness. Ahhaa transforms and positively impacts life quality. People often focus on the science of achievement. Ahhaa focuses on the art of fulfillment to be able to relate with people in our lives & find peace & happiness .

MARKET OPPORTUNITY

- World's 3.2B workers are unwell in mind, body and soul
- Expected market opportunity per year: $320B (Avg $100 spend), growing at 12%
- Target market: $ 160B (50% of total market)
- Available market in 0-3 years: $16B

PROBLEM

- People experiencing insecurity and stress due to economic issues, aging and health.
- Lack of tangible technology driven mind growth solution.
- No dedicated offline or online space to address the personal state of mind.
- Companies experiencing absenteeism and attrition.
- Lack of access to workplace wellness solutions.
- Credibility of program creators and deliverers in question.

SOLUTION

- Topic based 3-5 mins specially engineered inner growth programs for success, happiness & fulfillment.

- Uniquely designed by a former monk who has helped people from all walks of life in 42 countries.
- Easy access to immersive mind learning all the time.
- Dedicated Ahhaa space for workforce which combines Ahhaa VR & invigorating sensory inputs.
- Access in mins to 45 different global platforms where Ahhaa is already a trending channel.

VALUE PROPOSITION

Corporate / Organizations
Invest in the mental health of your employee:
- Increase Productivity
- Reduce Absenteeism
- Reduce Attrition
- Impactful Organizational Culture
- Be Known for being a great place to work
- Healthier & happier team spirits

Students become
- Mindful
- Compassionate
- Aligned with their core
- Passionate
- Better performers in studies & examination

For all Learners
Create a life full of happiness & fulfillment by
- Deeper sense of connection with your family and friends
- Higher growth & contribution
- Extraordinary responses to life situations
- Inclusive thought, word & action

CURRENT TRACTION

- Ahhaa on 45 global digital platforms (including iTunes, spotify, gaana, saavn...)
- Prime Minister Modi experienced Ahhaa.
- Key Partnerships: Accenture, Google, Oracle, Litchi (300000 schools), Aditya Birla, HUL
- UN has joined hands to take Ahhaa global.
- Special Research with Harvard Medical School on "Mind & Medicine"
- Revenue: $60K for FY18, $200K for FY19F

PEOPLE INVOLVED

ASHWIN SRISAILAM	DIANE BACCHUS QUDDUS	KARAN GROVER	BEENA AMMANATH	AIRONG LI	DR. ARAVIND CHINCHURE
Co-Founder	Co-Founder	Business Growth Head	Tech Head & Advisor	Research	Growth

Abroad Shiksha

Abroad Shiksha is steadily multiplying revenues by increasing their digital platform reach. They are no more branded as just an overseas education counseling company. Their end-to-end solution of a career pathway, university search, overseas admission partnership, education loans, visa processing, insurance, and post-landing assistance makes them poised for a revenue jump that can easily beat any market estimate. Their VP has maintained a great balance between product development and focus on revenue.

Kanav Sachdeva started Abroad Shiksha in Delhi, along with his wife Jyoti Sharma, as an offline student advisory firm almost two years ago before realizing that taking the entire process online would help streamline it and reach out to a lot more people. Their technology is currently in beta mode with students who have already used their services and is not generating good traffic. At present, it has a few consultants on board, including Sachdeva, who assesses students based on some standardized psychometric tests. Jyoti manages operations for the company. The services offered range from helping students understand how to go about the admissions process to providing training for various tests and helping them with the application and visa process. Abroad Shiksha has tie-ups with 350 universities in the USA and 2,500 globally, and charges universities for admissions, taking a nominal fee from students for the various services offered. It earns its major revenue from the universities that it has marketing tie-ups with. Next, their plan is to focus on establishing the brand in India before taking it to countries such as Sri Lanka, Bangladesh, Vietnam, and the Middle East.

CONCEPT

A digital ecosystem connecting students with the best fit universities globally. Playing an instrumental role in helping students find higher education opportuinities.

MARKET OPPORTUNITY

- K12 / UG / PG students aspiring for overseas education. Around 300K students go abroad for further education from India
- The market has increased 10%-15% YoY basis over the last 5 years.
- Rise in middle class population and income levels. Thus more emphasis on quality education with rise in affordability.
- End to end solution in a blue ocean market.

PROBLEM

- Lack of validated & transparent information on education options available to students aspiring to go abroad.
- Highly fragmented foreign-education facilitation services market.
- Lack of direct interaction with the university officials abroad to streamline application process.
- Lack of availability of good counsellors in tier 3 and 4 towns.

SOLUTION

Technology progressive solution ensuring transparency and student career centric guidance.

- Ethical / transparent pan-India platform with globally scalable opportunity.
- Online / mobile based delivery model:
  - Streamlined processes.
  - Allow students to work on their own pace from the convenience of their home.
  - Increase student retention from initial call to final placement.
  - Bring the required transparency for students when choosing higher educational opportunities abroad.

BUSINESS MODEL

- Success fee from Universities
- Test Prep fee from Students
- Consulting and application process fee
- Career Path exploration and assessment

VALUE PROPOSITION

Students

- Engage with students with the goal of getting them admissions and scholarships in premier universities abroad.
- Matching the best possible University and location for the students for their career aspirations.
- Online test prep classes to prepare students on various competitive/aptitude tests.
- Personalised career counselling
- Capable of placing any student directly into a premier University in countries like USA, UK, Singapore, Canada, Australia, NZ, Ireland, Malaysia, Germany, Ukraine, Switzerland, Poland.

Universities

- Serves as the complete international student recruitment solution for any foreign university.
- Help universities promote and market themselves across student population at schools, colleges and training institutes.
- Serve as universities' own in country representatives and ensure right network / channel creation to drive student recruitment.

CURRENT TRACTION

- Have already sent 500+ students abroad with another 100+ in the pipeline.
- Generated $950K + revenue
- An associate network available throughout India
- Counselled over 12000+ students for career planning, IELTS preparation.
- Working with 1000 + foreign universities / across 48 countries & growing
- Incorporating AI based solutions for university recomendation and counselling

PEOPLE INVOLVED

| KANAV SACHDEVA | JYOTI SHARMA | MANISH UPADHYAY |
| Founder | Co-Founder | Venture Partner |

EDAPT

Rebranded as EDAPT, KnowHassles provides a complementary service with Abroad Shiksha. It is important to note that the founder has an objective focus on revenue, and has achieved revenues in the first year of operations. Now with our ecosystem, tech partnerships, overseas relations, and team development are being strengthened.

EDAPT
Mumbai, India

CONCEPT

Founded by a problem solver, hustler & serial entrepreneur, KnowHassles EdApt intends to provide just the right solutions to international students' everlasting problems related to settlement in a foreign land in the form of mobile app.

Web based platform creates an ecosystem for International students, offering them a combination of vital information about necessary on arrival processes, social networking based value added services, student specific product marketing & e-commerce shopping experience.

MARKET OPPORTUNITY

- Approximately 3 Lakh indian students are seeking foreign education every year in various countries like the US, the UK, Canada, Australia, New Zealand, Germany, etc.
- According to World Education News and Reviews (WENR), the trend of indian students traveling abroad is rising by 21% each year.
- India has very good mobile phone adoption 57% of its population using at least one cell phone.
- Moreover, Google India serves nearly 90,500 monthly searches related to foreign education.

PROBLEM

- Least emphasis given on international students' settlement queries by education consultancies abroad.
- Inadequate knowledge shared about important processes by the counsellors.
- Necessary services and goods scattered on different web portals.
- High dependency on facebook friends & social media groups for all the solutions.
- No timely responses to urgent queries.

SOLUTION

- Settlement related quality digitize information on handheld devices.
- One stop shop for goods and services that cater to every need, saving time and money.
- Features like dynamic discussion board get quick responses from the experts.
- Enhanced value added services like roommate finder presenting all new experience of networking communication and match-making.

PEOPLE INVOLVED

We provide services for survival in Toronto

Register with us and be tension free

Family like environment overseas

VALUE PROPOSITION

For students:
- All goods & services under one roof.
- Roommate finder to find perfect match.
- Quick answers to their questions.
- Promotional offers and coupons to avail discounts.
- Peace of mind while in new country.

For Businesses working in tandem:
- Country wise segregation of students to sell products accordingly.
- Inexpensive platform to promote products to the target market.
- Branding , surveys and promotional activities on the app.

CURRENT TRACTION

- Service model implemented in Toronto and Berlin
- More than 70 students served
- Revenue of $15K generated in first year
- Partnered with Edwise International
- Delivered pre-departure seminars in KC College - Mumbai, Symbiosis International University - Pune, Surat, Vadodara and Ahmedabad.
- More than 50 education counsellors trained
- Associated with more than 10 service providers

HARSHAD WALHEKAR
Co-Founder

HARSHAD MAHAJAN
Co-Founder

Vidya Robotics

Vidya Robotics is founded by a serial entrepreneur. Along with his VPs, their product is being molded to world-class level. However, the first objective was to pilot it in schools and soft launch a paid project. It is good news that everything is going in the right direction for them.

Vidya

CONCEPT

Founded by a tech-enthusiast, developer and trainer since last one decade, Vidya Robotics is an electronics and Robotics Education company which is developing a host of educational robots and online training courses for children's edutainment. Our products aim at enhancing STEM skills in young minds above 8 years and making learning a fun activity for them. Using principles of Robotics, AI & IoT, help children receive an early exposure to technology, coding and electronic hardware. Vidya Robotics aims at bridging the gap between application-based quality learning and available robotics toys/tools

MARKET OPPORTUNITY

As per 2011 census of India, there are a total of 24.67 crore children in the age of 5 – 17 years who attend formal schools. With the rising disposable income in metropolitan and tier 2 cities of India, backed by our training experience and educated guesstimate is that a recurring market of over 25 lakhs children aspire to purchase robotics learning course and robotics hardware tools every six months in India. Moreover, with the abruptly changing technology, there are new robots and new technologies to learn almost every new year giving us a very big opportunity to provide Robotics Education under single roof.

PROBLEM

Robotics Education, while not new in this age, many kids and parents don't find a proper way to introduce these technologies to their kids. And robotics is surely limited to school labs or workshop organizers.
Kids who are highly interested in learning technology are limited by the availability of classes around them or in schools.
The current need is to provide learning tools that facilitate education staying at home while developing skills of growing kids. Vidya Robotics tends to close this gap and bring the technology education straight to the home with the help of online learning and easy to use DIY tools, which can be purchased directly.

SOLUTION

Vidya Robotics is developing an online platform which is a one stop solution for robotics and technology learning. This is an e-learning platform which hosts different learning modules / courses around technology and also act as an ecommerce platform for buying tools to experiment with Robotics and Technology. We've also developed an educational robot called 'Playme'.

It provides a fun experience while learning programming and kids can utilize their hours of free time in solving programming challenges on the robot. Additionally, it makes science, electronics and programming lessons fun to learn.
Vidya Robotics is developing different training courses depending on different age groups and technology domains. One can buy any of the tools / training modules directly from the website anytime.

BUSINESS MODEL

Vidya Robotics will charge per training module sold through our website. The training modules are priced individually and have a lifetime access once purchased. Along with training modules, Vidya Robotics gets revenue by the hardware products that are sold through platform for completion of these trainings. So, a person coming to buy a training course can buy the needed hardware from our store itself. Later, even if he doesn't want another training course, he can visit us for buying more products/ tools. The attractive pricing of the training modules will ensure accessibility to a wide spectrum of customers and access the online community we're building around Robotics.
The company plans to introduce various robotics trainings and products in due course to target different segments along with an online forum where children can participate in various challenges within their age groups or communities.

VALUE PROPOSITION

- First of its kind one-stop place for everything related to Electronics and Robotics Learning
- Equally usable for people from age 6 to 60
- First Online learning platform coupled with hardware store
- In-house Product development
- Third Party Product Sales
- Community for Robotics for many possible business opportunities

CURRENT TRACTION

- 7 years of experience in executing 2000 electronics based projects and over 5000 students trained.
- Successfully built MVP and sold 35 Robots to our existing customers for concept validation & feedback
- Built and sold 2 online training courses to 14 students through Udemy

PEOPLE INVOLVED

| AMIT RANA | PRATIKSHA KASBEKAR | ATINDRIYA BOSE | ROHIT LALWANI | MANISH UPADHYAY |
| Founder | Embedded Programmer | Venture Partner | Mentor | Venture Partner |

Often when I sit and discuss revenue with companies, the discussion leads to the idea of growing the base first and then trying to convert users into paying customers. However, it is clear that one can get a million hits for free services but the moment money is involved, the numbers start to slow down. Founders keep stressing that revenue drives growth, while there are others who conclude that user growth drives revenue.

Every startup dreams of achieving that milestone when they can focus more on scaling the business and enjoying their earnings rather than struggling for another infusion of investment. Most are still confused about the right priority. Should they focus on increasing revenues and profitability, or entice more and more users with freemiums to increase valuation?

Simulanis stands apart in their focus on revenue, steadily moving from ₹2 lakhs per month in 2016–17 to closing at ₹7–8 lakhs per month 2017–18 onwards. Having also won the National Entrepreneurship Award (Education) 2017, they are poised to create a great organization.

SPOTLIGHT: Simulanis

The widening gap between the skills required by businesses and the practical knowledge of a large number of engineering students got Raman Talwar started on his entrepreneurial journey. With an aim to help bridge the skills gap through the aid of advanced technology, this 28-year-old engineering graduate founded Simulanis in November 2013. "The foremost inspiration to start this company was my passion for building computer-aided simulation models that mimic real-life processes, followed by the desire to solve the challenging problem of the large unskilled population in our country," says Talwar, founder and CEO of India's most awarded edtech company.

The company started out as a skills training enterprise that delivered computer-aided design and training services to engineering students. It subsequently branched out to provide simulated work environments to help train professionals as well. In 2015, they reoriented to a product-based model and started working on AR and VR technologies that addressed the pain points faced in engineering education and industrial training.

Today, Simulanis harnesses AR and VR technology to help companies across various industries—pharmaceuticals, automobiles, FMCG, and manufacturing—train their staff. It continues to work in the engineering education sector, and has developed applications that assist students in visualizing and thus understanding challenging subjects and concepts. Their products help students and trainees learn difficult concepts easily and interactively through immersive AR/VR and 3D gamification methods. Simulanis' offerings include *Saral*, an AR learning platform, and *Protocol*, a gamified learning platform. This diversification is a result of EDUGILD realigning Simulanis' focus from being an AR-led book publisher onto more global opportunities. Raman has already registered his company in the UK as well, and will soon be scouting for opportunities there.

The company, founded with an investment of ₹15 lakhs, put in by the founder, has faced several challenges—from building their team to setting up their office and acquiring their first customer. Developing a viable product in the most frugal manner was among their biggest challenges, especially when a lot of it was undone during their stint at EDUGILD.

Faring quite well in its first year of operations, Simulanis saw its top line shrink in 2015–16 and corrected its course to offer a wider bouquet of skills training, moving on to AR/VR tech-enabled products. The shift in the business model helped the company get back on track. The change in strategy also drew investor interest. Apurva Chamaria (Chief Revenue officer @ Rategain, ex Vice-president and Head of Corporate Marketing HCL Technologies) and US-based venture capital firm Village Capital have invested in Simulanis. In 2016–17, it achieved ₹62 lakhs in revenue. Although the number is still modest, the startup is now set on a faster growth trajectory.

Since 2016, Simulanis has also won several awards including the Science and Technology Entrepreneurship, Innovation, Strategic and Leadership Excellence Award from the National Science and Technology Entrepreneurship Development Board of the Government of India, Tech Business of the Year 2016 from ASSOCHAM India, and Global Edtech Startup Award 2016 for Asia. Now they work with leading pharma, oil, and gas companies in the country for skill development and enhancement. Ultimately, the money infused by the investors was a pure play of the revenue capability that Raman demonstrated with the Simulanis team.

The pendulum of investor assessment is swinging back, with them looking for indications of business integrity, stability, and growth. The path of freebees and trying to create a critical mass at the cost of investors seem to be fading out steadily. Along with revenue, the bottom line or gross margin is very important for the ecosystem's stakeholders. So a revenue-enhancing business with consistently growing margins at a unit economics level seems like the right framework for success. To enhance productivity, startups also need to consider low cost of customer acquisition, high retention, repeat purchase, and high revenue per employee, through their ability to cross-sell and upsell. High customer churn rate still remains a strong indicator of a high-risk opportunity.

Feed self, then get fed: get your revenues on the table and then approach an investor for funds. The reverse action will lead to a short-lived organization.

CHAPTER 9

Being Investible

Investment philosophy generally changes with respect to the different life cycle stages of a company. During seed/early stages, there is little quantitative information to make a sound decision, and hence valuation at this point becomes more of an art than a science. During Series A funding stage and beyond, the company has already validated its business model and is in the growth phase, and hence a more accurate valuation can be performed—the factors that are considered during the early stages would already have been validated, and some additional factors would be considered. In my current portfolio, most of the companies raised money to sustain their needs initially through friends and families, then high net worth individuals (HNWIs), and finally through recognized funds.

One gentleman who stood apart in our relationship is Sachin Tagra, a seasoned professional, investor, VP, and think tank to EDUGILD as well as a larger mass. This chapter highlights his experience as a VP and progresses to evaluate companies from an investibility perspective.

Most of Sachin's career has been in a business-operating role. That is, he has always run businesses with the objective of scaling up and making money. His first job was in a sort of startup in the FMCG space funded by a large Indian FMCG company in partnership with a French MNC in the cheese category. He quite liked the startup environment of getting involved in the many key important decisions required for businesses to grow and the opportunity for faster growth. As he comes from a lesser known business management school background and not from an IIM, both these aspects were important for him to grow faster. Hence, he started preferring to look for opportunities in newly formed companies or businesses, which were well supported by large corporates. The concept of disruptive startups in India funded by venture capitalists did not exist in the late 1990s. Fortunately, he managed to land jobs in the formation stages of the businesses. So Sachin became a startup guy for a different model, with less dependence of external investors and low probability of funds drying up soon. His current job also entails setting up an investment business for a large corporate, and he thoroughly enjoys this early phase of the business.

Sachin visits incubators, accelerators, and co-working space as a mentor to interact with startups. He either conducts group sessions on fund raising or spends one-to-one time as a mentor. In group sessions, he generally discusses fund raising by startups followed by a question and answer round. He provides insights on investor perspective without going into too much detail, which will help the startups raise funds in the future.

In the one-to-one sessions, startup founders explain their business to Sachin and expect him to answer their queries related to business idea, team, execution, fund raising, etc. These sessions last for from 45 minutes to an hour. The founders get some answers in these sessions but they then start comparing his views with those of the other advisors they have met, and, as far as Sachin can make out, it will always be a challenge for the founders to absorb different views and decide on the final action. In the startup world, execution is any day more important than the idea. So taking advice from many mentors can actually lead to more confusion rather than clarity.

In early 2016, I reached out to Sachin and explained to him the vision of EDUGILD and the way they want to build this platform. I also explained to him the *venture partner model*, which is an arrangement in which one mentor is attached to the startup as a guide and sounding board throughout the journey of scale up, which may be 1–2 years at least, and not just an hour of interaction. In this model, the mentor also becomes an equity partner by contributing his/her time, experience, and network to facilitate the startup venture.

At that time, Sachin was also helping another startup as the solo mentor or advisor, and that gave him a good insight as to why startups need mentors. Sachin met the top 70 *ET Power of Ideas* startups at the 2015 residential mentoring session at IIM Ahmedabad. They had the best of the entrepreneurs and mentors visiting them in the 10-day session, but were still not clear on the strategy and guidance required to scale up. So, their very clear need was a sounding board member who will guide them as well as bring along his/her knowledge and industry connects—a need that was not fulfilled merely by listening to all the experts. So, Sachin's interaction with this startup (mentioned earlier) and my request to him led to him taking the call to become a VP with EDUGILD.

Initially, when EDUGILD started as an accelerator, they had three startups (including ClassBoat) attached to them, all in very different domains but very similar stages of development. I made

Sachin interact with all these startups and created an "arranged marriage" like environment between the startups and VPs. *It had very less or no dating involved.* It was a critical exercise for EDUGILD, as the acceleration model was based on the learning relationship of the startups with VPs. Both the parties had never interacted with each other before, and now the startup had to start sharing almost every key detail of their business with them. This was the beginning of the phase to start trusting the VP and ask for their guidance in answering all their business-related questions.

Sachin eventually became the VP of ClassBoat, and we learnt the important lesson that being investible starts with being able to attract the best advisory ecosystem. It cuts short your learning curve toward building a company that would garner investors' interest. ClassBoat was founded by husband–wife duo, Jay and Renu, of consulting and IT backgrounds, who moved from London to Pune with high hopes and dreams to disrupt the Indian education market. They came with the vision of building a platform for making the discovery of hobby classes easy for parents, which would also be an efficient lead generation tool for class providers. The idea was simple and had the potential to become large.

Sachin's journey with ClassBoat started with both parties understanding each other first as people, through a formal call initially and then a personal meeting. Sachin claims that initially he was not sure of the space in which ClassBoat was operating, as many were trying to solve the same problem, a couple of them already scaling up fast. Also, their unclear monetization strategy was not giving him confidence. But the good things Sachin noticed were their openness, flexibility, intelligence, and most importantly passion to make it work. Hence, he decided to contribute toward their scale-up journey. The decision was not that difficult to take, as there was no monetary risk involved for Sachin except the time he was contributing, which is what led him to become their VP. The other reason to go ahead was also to be a core part of the EDUGILD journey.

ClassBoat were at the stage of building a new product and platform, with reasonable clarity on the product construct but not too much of a clue on the monetization front. Building the business with a hazy picture of its monetization was a bit dangerous for the startup, and Sachin is a firm believer of making some money in every transaction (bit by bit, making the company investible and self-fed). So I guess it was a "good match" of sorts.

Interactions between Sachin and ClassBoat started with scheduled calls on a weekly basis, and sometimes in between the week, depending on their need. They started discussing product construct, ways to acquire class providers, digital marketing, strategy to hire, cash flows, investor pitches, and of course the possible ways to monetize this business and make money. The interactions became more productive and intense over a period of time. Sachin started getting the feeling that they were progressing well. ClassBoat founders started traveling to Mumbai often to ensure that they met face-to-face at least once every fortnight, and Sachin would travel to Pune once every month for the intervention. Often Sachin and the founders had a marathon meeting of six hours or more. It was about building a detailed financial plan for three years, carrying out a cost-benefit analysis, marketing management, etc. Building a plan like this involves capturing all the variables of the business and defining the assumptions.

As a result of one such 6-hour meeting, they managed to build the framework, structure, and the model, listing all the key assumptions. It was one of the longest meetings for these folks in some time. Over the next few weeks, they closed on the plan and the founders developed the confidence to talk about the same with external stakeholders—customers, mentors, and investors. The founders started working with MS Excel to build the various scenarios of the expansion. Sachin could clearly see the change in the confidence of the founders in discussing numbers with me and other stakeholders.

It progressed well during the first few months of acceleration, but they did not see much traction with the VC funds and the revenue did not scale up as expected. The business continued to burn money, which led them to start focusing on cash burn reduction/optimization to remain afloat. They reduced some fixed expenses, but going below a certain level was difficult. The entire focus shifted to generating revenue, thanks to Sachin's reviewing the revenue. This was the lucky moment when we all realized that being investible is not just about money but it is also about the capability to attract time investment from people like Sachin. It was tough for ClassBoat to change their direction but I guess they also realized that it is important for their survival. In this phase, they also pondered over who will be their paying customers and where should they focus their energies to realize revenue. The EDUGILD team with their deep education industry experience helped them in this realization, and they changed their model to focus on high-ticket courses by institutes and not just individual class providers. Although individual class providers continue to exist on the platform and some forward-looking class providers continue to pay them for the leads, they are not the majority today.

Working out a monetization model was tough for ClassBoat, but they were always good in generating leads. This was their strength from the beginning, which continued to be so. Their lead generation strength helped them bring on board a large angel investor from the education space. He was their customer, and decided to invest with a strategic objective. The investor also offered them six months of working space free of charge. So, the bootstrapping also started helping the organization focus on the important aspects of revenue and investibility. All this while, and till date, Sachin remains the sheet anchor for ClassBoat and the relationship is strengthening by the day. I manage to meet ClassBoat once a month and they take advice from Sachin more often than that. On his part, Sachin has always expressed the desire to support and be available, and we seem fortunate to have him in our network. I met Sachin recently; he has undergone a major surgery. However, once the courtesies were over, he was keen to discuss about what was happening at EDUGILD and ClassBoat. That is the way he is—*a man of steel.*

Presently, ClassBoat's business is generating cash on a monthly basis in the Pune market, and they are ready to expand to Mumbai, Bangalore, and the NCR. They also got a couple of angel investors to be a part of their journey, and this happened when they achieved breakeven. Sachin's interaction with them has caused them to reduce on tactics, and the general discussion now is about expanding profitably to other cities. It is no more about staying afloat. Finally, they have found their direction, which will take them far.

During this process, Sachin also got the opportunity to interact with three VPs who were senior industry leaders and experts in their domain. He claims to have learnt from their interaction with ClassBoat and their other mentee startups. He did not expect this *venture partner model* to be his learning platform too, but that is how it turned out to be.

Assessing the Investibility Potential of Companies: Why a Mentor's Background Matters

Sachin moved to the investment world in 2014 with The Times Group's strategic investment arm Brand Capital. It does not involve pure cash investing like a venture capitalist, but the investment process works very similar to a VC fund and may involve more risk. His role was to set up a new business/investment model for the Group. As Sachin was always passionate about startups, he proposed a different investment model for very early stage businesses, which was not the focus area then for Brand Capital. They called it *Incubator Capital*.

Sachin then started getting deeper into the startup space through early stage investment platforms, accelerators, and incubators, and started interacting with several startups looking for funding. Some ideas were both very unique and disruptive, and solved real problems existing in our community, but most of them were copies of ideas of some successful startups—run-of-the-mill. Some startups were solving problems but did not have the potential to make money; in fact, they had the recipes to lose money and time.

So it was important for Sachin to set up his thesis and evaluation criteria and not get swayed by what was happening in the investor world around. And he considers himself a conservative investor. There are no ideal answers for what is right when you are investing. You are taking a call for the future based on the information available presently and your view on the potential of an idea.

In Sachin's golden words, "The most important criteria to evaluate a startup are the founder's passion, their clarity of thoughts and perseverance, and whether they can make money for you.

Investors are investing to generate return for their funds and to be part of the journey." Sachin asks the following questions to filter any idea:

- Is this idea solving any unmet need of consumers/businesses?
- Will customers pay for it?
- How much will they pay for it?
- How many such customers are possible?

Sometimes the answers to these questions are not clear but the founder is willing to learn quickly and find the answers. Sachin has been classifying startups into three categories, explained here, which have different evaluation criteria; sometimes there is an overlap, so the filters adjust accordingly. It is needless to mention that all the three categories have to have some innovation in their product or service, which solves the unmet need of some consumer segment.

- *IP-led businesses:* Businesses that have developed some core technology that has the potential to get "patented", that is, it is "not easy" to develop similar technology. The key aspect of this evaluation is to understand the technology in detail, who has developed it, and why it cannot be copied in the next 1–2 years. Monetization is dependent on the size of the market they are addressing and the speed at which they are able to acquire a significant customer base in the next two years. Most of these businesses have the potential to be acquired by large tech companies and big corporates. Also, they can exist as standalone businesses with the opportunity to charge premium pricing.
- *Engagement-led businesses:* Businesses that are generating or have the potential to generate engagement but monetization is distant and unclear. Evaluation is on the basis of the number of consumers using the service and how many times they are using

it in a month/week/day. Sometimes the current numbers are less, but as an investor, one has to be aware of the hypothesis of the engagement. These businesses are primarily in the media and gaming segments. WhatsApp is the best example of this category. They need significant fund-raising initially and the revenue follows much later.

- *Pure commerce-based businesses:* Businesses that are into selling products and services. This is generally the largest segment in India. As a country, we have many challenges in every-day life and thereby associated opportunities. E-commerce, taxi services, food delivery services, home services, etc., are all examples of this category. It is easier to evaluate such businesses, as one can relate to their products and services based on individual needs. The first metric is to understand whether a particular need is currently serviced or not. If yes, then by whom and whether it can be organized and served in a better manner than the existing delivery model. Second, is the startup making money on every transaction? Even a small amount is good, but it has to have positive unit economics. Imagine if the business were to lose money on every transaction, the loss would get multiplied with the scale. Cash loss on every transaction works only until external investors are funding the business. In the last three years, we have seen many examples where the business has not been able to raise funds because of change in the funding environment and the appeal of the business fading with time.

Another way to evaluate is to see if the current delivery model can be disrupted and is there money to be made by adding value to the current model. Both e-commerce and taxi services are perfect examples. They add to the convenience of the consumers at the same or better pricing. This category of business also involves significant effort in marketing and brand building.

Sachin highlights that there is no right answer when you are deciding whether to invest or not. Many investors have missed large value creation opportunities and an equal number of investors have lost money by investing in failed startups. It is all based on your understanding and gut feel, which is a combination of both art and science. The proportion of art and science varies for each investor.

While I was fortunate to get Sachin's perspective on investibility, my dialog with the founder of MuseIn gave me interesting insights from a startup's perspective. According to Goutam, investors evaluate companies based on the following elements, which are some of the factors that need to be considered while evaluating an early-stage company:

- *Industry/sector*

    ○ Does this sector fall in the interest area of the venture capitalist? A venture capitalist would be more comfortable investing in sectors they have had brief experience of and some knowledge about.

    ○ Other venture capitalists interests in the sector.

    ○ Growth in the sector, propelling growth of startups.

- *PMF*

    ○ Novelty of the solution. Is the problem real and does the solution solve the problem?

    ○ Has the company interacted with enough customers to validate the PMF?

- *Market opportunity*

    ○ What is the available market opportunity? A solution addressing a large-scale problem has the ability to scale up.

- Is the solution scalable at a faster rate (through tech and other levers)?

- *Competitive advantage*
  - What is the existing competitive landscape? Are there few players or is the market crowded? Is the market big enough to accommodate multiple players?
  - Does the company have enough moat over competition, through technology, IP, customer experience (CX) and loyalty, first mover advantage, business model, etc.?

- *Traction/revenues*
  - What are the current revenue/user and the growth metrics for the past few months?
  - What are the engagement metrics?
  - What is the cost of acquisition versus the loan-to-value (LTV) ratio of the customer?

- *Team*
  - This is one of the most crucial factors during early-stage evaluation. Do the founders genuinely believe in building the startup? Does the team have enough skills to run the startup? Do they have previous experience of working with/ building startups? These are some of the key factors to be evaluated by the venture capitalist.
  - Pedigree provides a sense of comfort but does not always help.

- *Financial projections*
  - The financial projections provided by the company must be validated.

- ○ Are the financial projections (revenue and growth) metrics realistic?
- ○ Does the expansion plan make sense? Is it too big to chew or not aggressive enough?

- *Investment and valuation*

  - ○ Is the investment ask in the ticket range of the VC fund? What are the ticket sizes and percentages of recent deals in similar space?
  - ○ Percentage stake should typically be in the range of 15–30 percent.
  - ○ Are other investors interested in co-investing?
  - ○ Exit multiples should be in range of 10×–20× for early stage and 3×–5× for late stage.

From outside, it seems that being investible is a gut feel of the investors; however, it is a science we all must understand.

Most of the companies I have worked with start with one or two founders as core team members and race to raise an MVP. This is relatively easy, as they put in their sweat and cash to build the product. However, they need money to take the product to the market, and funds for people and marketing. It is important to ensure that as a company, you must have your pockets full for at least one year of running and not be dependent on external funding during this period. However, since money is needed, the first element is to have a scientific approach to arriving at valuations and being able to justify it.

Valuation is an important part of investibility that is on the minds of a founder and an investor. Valuation matters to investors, as they are getting company shares for the money they are going to put into the company.

At a high level, if you are valued at ₹5 crores and an investor puts ₹50 lakhs into the venture, the equity of 10 percent is passed on. But this does not mean that the company has ₹5 crores. So the valuation at the seed stage is about the credibility of the founders and the promise or potential of growth in the near future. So, for early-stage companies, valuation is the science of predicting growth rather than immediate performance considerations.

Key Decision-making Points While Agreeing to a Valuation

- *The Sector:* When one investor takes the lead, it may attract other investors' attention. So, if there is a sector appearing as the flavor of the moment and a few investors take the lead, then others may also pitch in. Sometimes investors may pay a premium to be able to participate in the rounds in particular sectors.

- *Revenues:* Early revenues are music to the investors' ears. Moreover, this is a very favorable factor for the founders as well: A company having tasted revenue can stick to a valuation that is higher than a traditional valuation of sorts. If the company has a working product in the early stages and is generating sporadic revenue from the market, this could be the most crucial element that will positively affect the investor decision.

- *Credibility:* Investors put money on the people who are responsible for developing the business. So the credibility of the founders is very important. However, the founders must also evaluate the investors' credibility and their ways of dealing with companies in the past.

- *GTM:* Clarity on GTM channels is a big confidence booster for investors. It has to be combined with market potential. Even though the product might be in very early stages, having clarity on the channel of sales is important.

General Scientific Thumb Rules

- *DCF or NPV method:* This is a popular method for the valuation of early-stage companies. The DCF method considers cash flows expected to be generated in the future by a company and discounts them to derive a net present value (NPV). Uncertainties and inflation elements are worked out based on assumptions.

- *Exit expectation method:* Here, an investor assumes the amount they want to make when exiting. So they work backwards from a period of 6–7 years and express what would they want the valuation to be today, so that they get the value they expect at exit.

- *Competitive benchmarking:* This method attempts to estimate a valuation based on the valuation of comparable companies in the last two years. I advise my companies to ensure they raise enough funds for 18–24 months of need and not keep on going back to the market in shorter intervals. It takes a lot of time, money, and effort to start and close an investment cycle.

Finally, it is important to understand that macroeconomic and microeconomic factors greatly affect the valuation of a company. The PESTLE (political, economic, social, technological, legal, and environmental) aspects have to be circled back to regularly to check that all these elements are favorable to the business. Imagine a company launching materials in the education space that are soon made redundant through a directive from the regulators—it is a loss to all involved.

SPOTLIGHT: The Curious Case of Simulanis

Simulanis is our first batch company and we have been working together since February 2016. There are two reasons why Simulanis has always been investible: Raman the founder—he demonstrates unit economics growth month-over-month—and the space he is in. They were also the first EDUGILD company to raise a pre-Series A funding and the fastest one to do so. At the end of 2016, Simulanis raised pre-Series A funding from Village Capital and a consortium of angel investors. This was a follow through of the investments done in March 2016 by the mentors and advisors of EDUGILD.

Village Capital is an investment firm that finds, trains, and invests in early-stage entrepreneurs with business solutions to major global problems. The firm has made more than 75 early-stage investments in 15 countries. The consortium of angel investors referred to above includes Pawanjit Ahluwalia (Chairman, India Skills), Apurva Chamaria (Chief Revenue officer @ Rategain, ex Vice-president and Head of Corporate Marketing, HCL Technologies), and Mridul Upreti (CEO, Segregated Funds Group, Jones Lang LaSalle).

Simulanis was launched in November 2013 by Raman Talwar, a University of Manchester alumnus, with the aim to use AR and VR technologies to train engineering students and workforces through gamified content. Simulanis has developed hardware-agnostic, gamified mobile and computer training applications for the education, skilling, and industrial training sectors.

Simulanis initially picked up engineering textbooks and converted the data into gamified AR/VR applications, which students could access via Google Play Store or iOS. Occasionally, they also conducted workshop sessions in engineering colleges to enlighten students on the current state of AR/VR in the country and its applications in different sectors. However, when they landed in EDUGILD and I started working with them, we realized that the textbook model was about to put them in direct competition with established publishers. Such models are also not scalable and do not catch investors' attention. Hence, we advised reorientation, and Raman agreed to transform into a mixed-reality skill development solution provider, and thereafter the scale-up has been an unstoppable journey.

As the name suggests, Simulanis was conceptualized to simulate the real world the way we see it around us—right from the processes that are at the heart of industrial operations to human or automation activities that get those tasks executed in reality. What convinced the investors about Simulanis? They offer technology to provide corporations a clear path to reduce attrition and improve efficiency by better preparing workers in a much shorter span of time. They provide opportunities for individuals to build the skills to be competitive in a quickly evolving workforce.

Simulanis did not have it easy to their Series A. Being selected for the Village Capital bootcamp, they participated in their Education India 2016 investment-readiness program and got selected for investment by a group of peers.

With a team size of 30, the company is currently focusing on training the workforce in India in different sectors. It is currently working with two of the 10 biggest pharma companies (names undisclosed) to train their workforce in

India using AR/VR technology. Also, it claims to be in the process of training over 1,000 workers across multiple sites at present, and expects to be training 5,000 workers every year. The company is using the raised funds to expand its sales team in the pharma and automotive sector, while exploring other domains such as industrial goods, apart from education. The company is also conducting pilots with some automotive giants in the country to train their floor staff.

While investing in edtech and the likes of Simulanis, investors also keep an eye on the market potential. So, in this case, the indicators are very positive. The Indian education market is expected to almost double to $180 billion by 2020, according to a 2016 report by management consulting firm Technopak. On the other hand, until December 2016, the digital learning market was estimated to be at $2 billion and is expected to reach $5.7 billion by 2020. According to the National Skills Development Corporation, India will require 119 million more skilled workers by 2022 across 24 sectors in the economy. The cost-efficiency and efficacy of Simulanis' training solution, coupled with the scale, indicates well for them in a sector that's attracting more and more attention—again, making them investible.

The VR market globally is expected to touch $33.9 billion by 2022. "While Simulanis is currently getting a lot of traction in VR with the lucrative pharma and automotive sectors, I see VR implications in every industrial training use case," adds investor Apurva Chamaria. The sector has also witnessed active funding recently. To mention a few, in August 2016, edtech startup iAugmentor secured seed funding. Also, Genext Students, a technology-enabled student platform, raised \$209,000 (₹1.4 crores) from 1Crowd, a crowd-funding platform for startups. Prior to this, in March 2016, Bengaluru-based edtech startup Avagmah raised an undisclosed amount of funding.

So, according to our learning on investibility, the market size needs to be attractive enough to provide good returns for an investor. The startup should also have shown substantial traction, which can be identified in a variety of ways, such as, month-on-month growth or online sign-ups.

Take a look at how ClassBoat demonstrate their metrics, which is evidence enough of their traction—is it not solid? According to the founders, "What matters glaringly is the size of the market opportunity and the technology, which may have a first mover advantage or be futuristic."

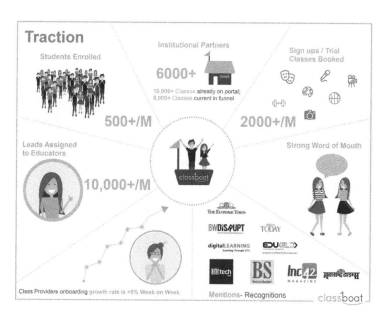

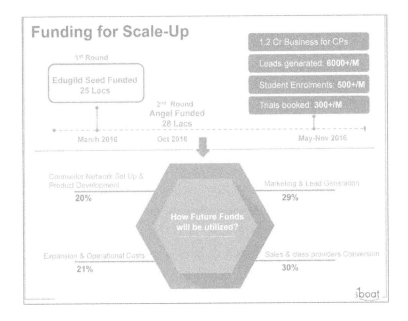

Here we will discuss how Hitesh, the founder of AmbitionUp, raised funding.

Hitesh Awtaney, CEO, says that, as of January 2017, his firm had raised enough capital to be able to grow to twice its current size. The good part is that he has lived up to his promises. He raised an undisclosed round of seed funding from investors in Dubai, primarily from friends and family. "The funds raised will be used largely toward building our internal capabilities in learning and development as well as in-house technology," Hitesh made a clear statement about the use of the funds.

Set up in early 2015, AmbitionUp is a career discovery platform and was part of the first batch of startups assisted by EDUGILD. Its vision is clear: It aims to provide personalized career recommendations to graduate students and helps them benchmark themselves to see what options are available at their current level.

The acceleration program at EDUGILD helped the company address the personalization problem, where graduates really need help to understand profiles and get an idea of where they stand. The company is engaged with actual professionals across career profiles to define employability through a "GradoScore" for each profile—a combination of technical skills, personality traits, and other parameters. This score allows graduates to benchmark themselves and see the jobs that are available at their current level, while also highlighting the tangible steps they can take (courses, workshops, mentorship, etc.) to improve their score and land better jobs. The company uses an affiliate revenue model apart from charging companies for recruitment, while the product stays free of charge for graduates. He added that the company would likely look for angel funding in a year from now.

These cases illustrate how the demonstration of perseverance and fortitude by the management team is important for investors. The bets are on the team first, which must be good. Moreover, I have witnessed investor–company meetings where the founders feel offended by the investors giving brutal feedback. This is not done. The founders must attend the meetings with a very constructive view and positive attitude. The level of enthusiasm is crucial. Investors claim that if the founders have built their company around a strong passion, then it undoubtedly has a brilliant future.

I have also come across entrepreneurs that create self-proclaimed timelines: "I want x amount of money in 30 days; make that happen." Well, they have a misconception that investors are going to invest straightaway. Practical advice to founders is to ensure they provide relevant data points for all the business aspects, which can lead to the investors fast tracking their decision-making process. Follow-ups with investors should not be to keep asking them about their levels of interest; instead, they should be followed up with meaningful and updated information on traction. It also seems that a startup's chances to raise funds are better if they have someone on the team with prior entrepreneurship experience. While this is not a must-have, it definitely adds brownie points.

What goes in favor or against a startup when they approach external stakeholders?

I have rarely seen startup founders sitting without distractions and trying to map what elements can give them leverage with external stakeholders and where they can poke holes. If done elementarily and properly, it brings about confidence during the founders' discussions with potential investors.

The Bitter and the Sweet of Seeking Funding

The Bitter

- *The uncertainty:* This happens at two levels, of which the first one is the legal and compliances (hygiene) discipline of the company and the second is the uncertainty in the sector of operation, that is, if the startup is in an industry that has recently shown poor performance or may be dying off. This specifically happened initially with YoScholar. Their business was growing fast, but, being branded as e-commerce, few investors would not even listen to them. Even Ahhaa.com had its initial difficulties where product differentiation had become a very difficult proposition. Gabe, the founder of Edorble, has been going through this uncertainty, since online learning enablement seems to have taken a setback in the fancy of investors. The positive element is that the drying up of investor interest pushes the startup founders to a new level of challenge, and they actually do not just face it but also come up with innovative ideas to remain bootstrapped.

- *Competition:* A red or a blue ocean? I have witnessed investor calls where the potential investor knew all about tech. The investor somehow made the startup confess that they knew little about the tech part. However, in the hindsight, the technology involved had less or no impact on the consumer experience. The proposition was not being sold on differentiated tech. However, despite being in a blue ocean, the startup got branded as being a part of a market that had cutthroat competition. Eventually, there were other believers in the company's business and its financial needs were met at the right time and in the right quantum.

- *Management fluidity:* This aspect is related to the founders' reputation and credibility. I have worked on this aspect and realized that if there is a strong management team, then the PR and publicity should reflect the same. I have also come across conversations where potential investors gave feedback that they are completely sold on the product, industry, and business model. However, they will not invest due to lack of confidence in the founders' and the team's capability to pull it off until it becomes a sizeable business. The psychometric and cognitive abilities of the founders have a lot to do in this aspect of confidence building. If the startup has lost founders/co-founders early in the journey, this also sends a negative message to the investors.

- *A "dead-on-arrival" (DOA) product:* A DOA product is a sin. Never take a product that does not work to an investor, and dare not call it a prototype. Investors do not give many shots to a proposition. So if the product fails to work when being demonstrated, no matter how good the idea is and its industry potential, it demonstrates lack of seriousness and groundwork on the part of the founders and in the startup's overall way of addressing stakeholders' interest.

- *Desperation:* Whenever I have heard that "we will shut down if the money does not come in three months," it has been a nervous time. I would rather prefer a company telling investors that "we may not grow as fast as we expect to or may scale down a bit if the investment comes late." It is all about the choice of words that conveys whether the founders are desperate or have the right backup plans if the money does not come when it is required.

The Sweet

- *Customer traction:* It is unarguably the biggest factor in justifying and place holding the valuation of the company. Having customers is a situation that boosts the investors' confidence to positivity. ChangeMyPath and AmbitionUp are garnering customers, refining their product to perfection, and thereafter will be making the shift from having on-boarded users to making them ready to pay for the services and experience. KidsTriangle has garnered 20+ pre-schools where their services are being used, and it is only a matter of time before they move and make the habit a paid utility.
- *Reputation:* Even if you are a first-time entrepreneur, you can create a reputation through your achievements, for example, in corporate life. Company founders such as those of ClassBoat

could boast of success in their 15 years of corporate stint, exposure in 12 countries, and successful food venture. Ashwin of Ahhaa.com lays emphasis on his monastery life, which makes the content that he creates seem to be extremely credible. Hitesh of AmbitionUp has the backup of being from a family of entrepreneurs. Basically, if one wants, there can definitely be avenues for startup founders to establish their reputation based on their current or erstwhile track record.

- *Having a showcase:* Getting funding for just an idea is impossible in the current environment. The founders must at least reach the prototyping stage before investors will even have the urge to talk to them. I have seen this in the case of StudyMarvel and Edvantics. Both are coming up with great propositions in the AR and learning analytics space, respectively. However, potential investors have asked them to be prototype-ready as a first step.

- *Revenue, music to the founders' ears:* Having customers is great news, but having *paying customers* is nirvana. It is much easier to understand valuations and justify the same when there is money coming into the company. I have personally seen this happening in the case of Simulanis, ClassBoat, Ahhaa.com, AmbitionUp, Abroad Shiksha, EDAPT by KnowHassles, and YoScholar, who have all got early and steady revenues. It may not be an assurance to get funded; however, the ground rules of the process for approaching investors are well set if the company starts making early revenue.

- *How much to ask:* There have been contradictory experiences here; no two are in agreement. If a startup specifies the amount they need and the potential investors are not willing to shell out the same, the startup valuation seems to dither. It requires a fine balance, where a startup must know what are they demanding and why; it should be based on rationale and logic, not on some quick work on numbers. The investors' willingness to invest and the startups' urge to attract the investment have to meet midway. If the balance does not exist, then it can be a very discouraging experience. I have worked with companies where the numbers were made more realistic and justifiable based on how the business and organization is expected to grow in a competitive environment and not in ideal conditions.

- *The flavor:* If a particular sector is booming and is in the news regularly, investors are more likely to pay a premium on the valuations. It is no surprise then that in the edtech ecosystem, we are witnessing the mixed reality and AI-based solutions being better accepted in investor meetings, since these two tech elements are being talked about in every industry, not just in the education sector.

Last but not the least, every investor has their own behavior. Hence, my advice to startups is to ensure that they let potential investors know if the company founders expect something more from the investors other than finance. For example, some investors become facilitators, influencers, collaborators, and even mentors, some others remain critics. In the end, it is you who matters, since this is your dream on its way to becoming a reality.

10

Roots to Wings—Levitate: Becoming a Global Enterprise

In the present scenario, global economic integration has become a reality and presents enormous opportunities for the future of the society and startups. For startups, economic exchange at a global level can lead to economies of scale, reputation, cost savings, and increased revenue. More importantly, it also gives them a foothold to draw on the talents and insights of a global workforce and the happenings in various parts of the world. With the government creating new avenues for cooperation, our own Invest India and Startup India efforts are very much worth applauding. In order to make Indian companies globally competitive, the Startup India initiative offers certification to the applicants and compliance under nine environmental and labor laws.

Indian companies do not fare well globally when it comes to awareness and compliances to intellectual property rights (IPR). Here again, the Indian government initiative kicks in, bearing the IPR facilitation cost and providing 50 percent rebate on trademark filing. Startup India also aspires to deploy ₹10,000 crores worth of funds for investment into startups through *alternate investment funds*. It is true that startups have always flourished in countries where the government becomes a demand generator and facilitator. Startup India does that for our startups, with the central ministries/ departments/community and public sector unions (CPSUs) relaxing the condition of prior turnover and experience for micro and small enterprises. The initiative also offers income tax exemption for a period of three consecutive years on capital gains as well as on investments above *fair market value*.

Consider the pride we experience as Indians when we realize that Indian companies are making their mark on the global landscape. In this chapter, I will recount the experiences of several Indian startups that went on to make it big after the initial hiccups. These will serve as great lessons for aspiring startups to learn from.

A man must be big enough to admit his mistakes,
smart enough to profit from them, and strong enough to
correct them.
—John C. Maxwell

Simplilearn: The Founder's Experience

It was great to learn from the founders of Simplilearn about their *roots to wings journey*, taking the Indian entrepreneurship ecosystem to the world. An element of brilliance is visible in the company's journey toward being a global company since the day they began operations. It is about setting a vision and making it happen. What started as a blog to help project management professional (PMP) aspirants through audio and video tutorials in 2009 has today become one of the largest edtech companies that helps working professionals and enterprises train for the digital economy.

Simplilearn has been global since its inception. Having started with providing certification training in project management, it has expanded its course offerings to IT service management, IT security management, quality management, etc. The company started out by providing training through a blend of online and traditional classrooms.

Being a company that believes in innovation and likes to keep pace with the changing times, Simplilearn introduced a key milestone in 2015 on the learning product front called the Online Classroom Flexi-Pass, a revolutionary on-demand live instructor-led training solution. Flexi-Pass allows learners to attend unlimited real-time face-to-face online sessions with world-class trainers, unbound by their geographies and time zones. With this launch, Simplilearn made the bold decision of moving away from traditional classroom training to focus only on online self-learning and instructor-led classrooms.

The year 2015 was also significant with respect to establishing the company's presence in the USA. In April 2015, Simplilearn raised $15 million in Series C funding from Mayfield Fund, Kalaari Capital, and Helion Venture Partners. The funding was raised to allow the company to expand in the North American market. In the same year, Simplilearn acquired Market Motive, a digital marketing training leader based in Silicon Valley. The acquisition paved way for Simplilearn not to just foray into the digital marketing category, but most importantly to set up operations in North America to offer turnkey solutions to working professionals and college graduates who are trying to advance their careers in the region. The move also merged the promotion of Market Motive's digital marketing courses with the much fuller suite of professional certification courses from Simplilearn.

Further on, Simplilearn expanded its focus toward the enterprise training business as well in the USA, India, and the rest of the world. This move was made considering the growing requirements of enterprises to train their employees in digital technologies in the backdrop of automation and other evolving technologies. Today, Simplilearn works with over 2,000 enterprises, a list that includes Fortune 500 companies across sectors such as IT/ITES, media and entertainment, pharma, BFSI (banking, financial services and insurance), and so on. Owing to their focus on the enterprise training business, Simplilearn expanded operations in the USA further by setting up an office in Raleigh, North Carolina, in October 2017.

Currently, Simplilearn has a library of over 400+ courses across digital technologies, which need a network of 2000+ trainers, and has trained about 500,000 working professionals across 150+ countries.

Ahhaa.com: Demonstrating International Viability

Along with the initiatives taken at various levels, I have had the privilege to work with startups that are demonstrating cross-border viability. Consider Ahhaa.com, created with the sole mission to help people feel awesome. This is done through creating byte-sized easy content for people to listen, see, understand, experience, and immerse themselves into using the best of technology. Their two biggest cross-border challenges were *people management* and *legal affairs*. After my initial discussion with the founders, I helped them onboard LegaLogic, a law firm that advises EDUGILD, and since then their incorporation and dual taxation journey has been smooth. However, the roots-to-wings challenge with people, that is, getting the right people at the right time with the right commitment, remained. In the following paragraphs, I describe how the founders made that easy.

The founders, Ashwin and Diane, come from diverse backgrounds—Ashwin has been a monk for 17 years and lived a life of guiding people's lives all over the world toward inner clarity. Having started her entrepreneurial journey at the age of nine, Diane has worked in corporate America, and is now a mother of two. Both had no background of technology whatsoever, other than the simple act of sending and receiving emails. However, that never hindered their passion to learn what was necessary to make Ahhaa reach the masses. The main ingredient of Ahhaa.com is being unstoppable.

Also, it so happened that the right people kept emerging and volunteering to take the work forward. While both the founders had roots in different continents, they brought the world closer by creating something that is unaffected by geographical boundaries. Once people emerged around the founders, Diane and Ashwin always wanted even the team to journey with Ahhaa to a place of faith in the mission for human impact.

The team ranged from UI/UX designers to software developers to sales/marketing members, of whom some stayed for a while, some left a lot sooner, and it all depended on how much they could believe and know that eventually this will be their biggest pay-off for life. At that stage, since both the founders were completely bootstrapped, it was tough for them to offer big salaries. The question always was how to set a middle path between the needs of a growing company, the mindset of the workforce, the bootstrapping, and the larger aspect of helping humanity, especially when the operations were spread between India and the USA, and the team was also available across multiple locations.

This did lead to times when the team was too small and unequipped to handle the scope, which left them with an aspiration to grow soon and have a team that is big enough to cater to all requirements.

In this process, another learning also emerged—in today's age of technology, a virtual team can also be quite effective, considering all the audio–video media available to communicate. A sense of flexibility along with a clear vision helped their growth to continue regardless of any circumstance. Also, the mental well-being of the team is crucial, and since Ahhaa is in this very business, the impact all this had on the team members could be seen as the best investment for the times to come. According to Richard Branson, "Clients do not come first. Employees come first. If you take care of your employees, they will take care of the clients."

Another clear requirement was for the founders to be ready to wear different hats as required from time to time, with any work becoming a work of privilege. Today, Ahhaa is a team of 13 people and is at an emotional juncture. From here, they are poised to create a global organization, to which all their learnings as a workforce are going to add tremendous value. This family of 13 now juggles their time to help with technology, content creation, business growth, and customer relations.

ChangeMyPath: Building a Global Startup— Founders' Perspective

Another global potential company that I am working with is ChangeMyPath (CMP), based in San Francisco and moving to various parts of the world. Their matured founders have a great perspective on the way the company is embracing the future.

The information age as well as merging of digital technology with daily business activities have made communication across the globe inevitable for any company, whether established or in early stage. There has been and will continue to be cross-pollination of ideas, working methodologies, and, of course, technology among countries, established and new companies, and leading edge thinkers that transcend borders and other boundaries. With the globalized economy, businesses need to diversify their sources of workforce, capital, and other core elements to survive and flourish.

In the case of their starting up CMP, Zack, David, Eva, and the team knew that job skills training, and education more broadly, is an empowering force that can transform and modernize economies, and, in particular, give workers within these economies the opportunity to directly control the advancement of their careers.

From its inception, CMP has had a clear vision: re-engineered jobs skills training, where curricula can change and adapt quickly and easily, driven by real-world data from various sources and geographic locations.

- Individuals will know their skills and can articulate and use them to get the jobs they want.
- Employers will know what they need, and hire and train effectively based on those needs.
- Educators will understand, train, and effectively prepare individuals for the current and future demands of employers.

To achieve this vision of skilled employees ready for the global economy, they knew that they needed to develop a system that could integrate the continuously changing employer requirements and connect them more closely to the job skills development of each individual user. The ultimate goal was to make sure that their software aligns with the real reason why people get education and training, to get a job or to increase their marketability for jobs.

The barrier to that vision has been the education and training system itself. The industry is burdened by a rigid approach, where first the need is defined, followed by a request for proposals (RFP), a proof of concept, change orders (requiring amendments for change in scope of work or nature of work in the middle of execution of a plan), cycle times of 12 weeks, and ultimately, a bloated, inefficient, often boring regurgitation of the days-gone-by using PowerPoint slides that have bored us all to tears over the last decade. There had to be a better way, and CMP was inspired by other content-driven businesses to find it. Someone had to step in and be the broadly accessible technology layer, which led to the formation of CMP.

As they looked to the future, to launch and grow, it became clear that a multipronged approach was going to be necessary. According to the founders,

> We had decided that our home market of the US would be our launching pad. We have the credibility from our career histories, and the place to make that first splash would be here at home. But when we started to look at growth opportunities, it really came down to an impact and suitability analysis.

Admittedly, from an outside perspective, they saw the opportunity as follows:

- India has approximately 50 percent of its population below the age of 25 and more than 65 percent below the age of 35. This is the highest in the world. More than 350 million people in India are 10–24 years old.

- The education system is failing these people. One realizes that this statement may be controversial, but when you speak to business leaders in the country, they all have the same feedback. The current education system is graduating fewer and fewer qualified applicants and the employability gap is growing, not narrowing.

- Technology will have to be the solution. India has led the way on "leap-frogging" in terms of 3G and wireless Internet instead of wiring the country with copper wire. With deep segmentation prevalent based on language and culture, particularly in poorer regions, the bridge cannot be made by boots-on-the-ground brute force; technology has to provide some of the leverage to close this gap.

- Although it has a massive youth population—nearly one-third of all the citizens of the metropolitan areas in India are youth—20 percent of this urban population lives on less than USD 1 per day. While, empirically, the overall quality of life is improving rapidly in the country, some people are being left behind (anecdotally, e.g., the differences between the state of Maharashtra or Kerala and states such as Bihar).

Explicitly, CMP is a technology provider that uses a broadly accessible authoring platform to enable SMEs, curriculum developers and providers, publishers, and enthusiasts alike to collaboratively author job skills training content. In addition to content developed by corporates for training, the technology has been built with a collaborative authoring and consumption approach as part of its DNA to foster peer learning, social groups, and thus leverage the positive effects of group dynamics.

From a growth perspective, they did not view the revenue potential in India as distinctly advantageous, but did see the

224 Kites in a Hurricane

potential impact as disproportionately large, particularly given that the edtech investment space and ecosystem, while small in India, has remained active. In the USA, the investment community has been more cyclic with regard to edtech and it has created a "fits and starts" cadence that hampers both growth and success.

The connection between their mission and the demographic and skilling challenge in India is immediate. They can work in their wheelhouse, as technology builders and platform purveyors, impact the communities and populations that need it, and build their business at locations where they think the company can have the greatest positive impact.

Further, CMP uses a modern web stack that has enabled them to be mobile first, a key differentiator and one of the reasons why they rightfully think they can find success in India. With the ongoing mobile phone company war driving the price of data down (thanks to Jio!), the ubiquity of mobile devices all but guarantees that the next evolution in content delivery will be found in the palm of your hand. If India is going to truly engage and embrace its citizenry and the potential demographic advantage that it provides, while the rest of the world's population ages, the inevitability of mobile-first as a content strategy across industries is writ large, and CMP wants to help form, drive, and participate in that evolution.

Finally, their founders also have a proven track record in international business, specifically in India. Their CEO has spent a significant amount of time in India in the video game industry, and their chairman of the board has previously been active in the clean energy space in India. This has made it familiar and comfortable for the business to focus on India as its primary growth market.

CodersTrust: My Mount Everest (by Jan-Cayo Fiebig, Founder)

During the course of my involvement with these high-performance companies, one of my unforgettable moments is meeting Cayo, the founder of CodersTrust. His vision to have an impact on the world while being headquartered in Denmark was amazing and he has lived up to it. His narrative deserves a unique place in this book and it is filled with learning that can be imbibed.

My journey began with hosting an event for Richard Branson in 2014, where my co-founder Ferdinand pitched him the core vision of CodersTrust—providing student finance for freelancers in emerging countries. That night we not only received blessings from a man I look up to [Dr Yunus] but also formed a Joint Venture with Professor Dr Yunus and Grameen Foundation to start our operations in Bangladesh. We had backing from a Nobel Peace Prize winner [Dr Yunus], received funding from the Danish Development Fund, a rockstar team, and all the motivation in the world. I was ready to set the course to Bangladesh. What could possibly go wrong?

CodersTrust is my Mount Everest—8676 meters high, with the ambition to financially enable talented minds to become successful freelancers, regardless of gender, race, and social background. We have created the most affordable online workforce in Bangladesh by training more than 40,000 students to become freelancers, increasing their salaries from $2 to $8 per hour. The World Bank, UNDP [United Nations Development Programme],

WFP [World Food Programme], Rockefeller Foundation, and the government itself funded our program, further bringing CodersTrust to slums in India, refugee camps in Iraq, rural areas in Kosovo, and the outskirts of Somaliland. It was a true discovery of human ambition, injustice in life, and an opportunity to make a difference. I shall not tell you about the highest highs of my journey, but rather shed light on the darkest alleys—challenges that drained my energy and brought the company to the edge. Such reflections have provided a great learning for me, and may also guide you through stormy times, if ever faced.

Hurricanes appear in all shapes and forms and have the power to move mountains and shake the inner core. I would like to highlight two types of high-magnitude hurricanes that have hit CodersTrust—the visible hurricane that I saw coming from a distance and yet was unable to change its course of direction and the invisible hurricane that, with its sudden appearance, almost destroyed my inner beliefs and put an end to the company.

The Visible Hurricane

My first year in Bangladesh was marked by an exploration into the unknown. Understanding potential students, testing the educational model and failing in the attempts, and building a passionate team. My workday would start at 7:00 am, when Sultana, our Career Agent, came to begin her student counselling, and end at 1:00 am with Maruf, our lead developer, leaving "the office". All this was taking place at my apartment in Dhaka, which I shared with my team during the day and a few cockroaches at night. Even the honking cars, the energy cuts, the hours spent in traffic, and the loneliness could not stop my enthusiasm. I must, however, say that a smile flashes across my face when I hear another story of two tech entrepreneurs sharing the hardship of starting their tech company in a garage in Silicon Valley.

The days were not long enough to fill all the ambition and work into. Partnerships, platform development, marketing campaigns, recruiting, team development, and financial controlling kept my mind engaged. With a monthly burn rate of $40,000, our cash reserves faded away sooner than forecasted. Six months came down to three months, which quickly reduced to just four weeks worth of resources. A visible hurricane came straight at us. Forty employees and operations in Bangladesh, India, and Kosovo were soon to be hit by the sheer force of insolvency. While spending time, money, and personal effort into raising capital, there was no guarantee that these efforts will materialize and bring in investment. This was a restless time filled with anxiety and discomfort, but requiring strength and courage to motivate the team, grow the business, and pitch to investors. The hurricane came closer and all my efforts seemed to accelerate it rather than slowing it down. How to look ahead when your own house is burning? How to explain to an employee that there is no salary being paid out, which supports the cancer treatment of his/her mother? Such a big responsibility was not only upon me but also on my team and all students. Eventually, I had to let go of eight people, the whole team took a three-month salary cut, and the idea of India as a market was shot down. The visible hurricane has left its mark. At the same time, our first employee sued us for late salary payments, core documents were deleted from our Dropbox folder, and Russian hackers stole $10,000 from our online freelance account. I felt tested by the universe.

The Invisible Hurricane

What would you say if I tell you that a dozen of our own employees took our customers, our IP, our processes, and started competing with us from a street next to our own office? A punch in the face would have been gentler compared to my feelings then of disappointment, anger, and frustration. With a change in the country's leadership, local operations in Bangladesh underwent a transformation toward greater transparency and digitalization. Over the next few years, we created a strong team spirit with flat hierarchies based on the Danish working culture. A more performance-oriented culture provided motivation to the engaged and at the same time posed a threat to the old way of doing things. A cluster was formed within the team that did not agree with the new direction. Combined with an emotional temper and young exposed egos, an escalation was in the making. After screaming, crying, and blaming, 12 team members took our Facebook page with 300,000 followers hostage, called all students to leave CodersTrust, stole all of our content, and changed passwords for core services. Laws were broken, IP infringed, and employment contracts disregarded. Looking at the hostile situation and uncertain future lying ahead of us, our morale was at its rock bottom. A litigation would have felt right, stimulating a feeling of revenge and righteousness, but it would certainly not have stopped the bleeding, and would have taken away our focus and remaining energy.

How does one remain strong and anchored in the face of such a struggle? An invisible hurricane that I did not see coming, making all other challenges irrelevant.

After the Storm

Such events are discouraging in nature and certainly not worth advertising, yet so important to share. What have I learned from almost insolvency, a hostage-like situation within my Bangladeshi team, lawsuits, and mental distress? At the end, I learnt that a situation is never good or bad, it is how we perceive it. The lowest low can with time turn into the highest high. Clearly, the explained events were destructive in nature but also provided us with the opportunity to rise beyond ourselves. An organization that has survived such catastrophes grows stronger together, building the resilience and courage to look ahead. We were able to fill the vacant positions with talented bright minds that brought the experience and skill set required to grow and prosper. We established new initiatives that created healthy habits and formed a company of unity. Hence, it is no surprise to me that CodersTrust has just been awarded by the Danish Development Fund to train 7,000 young talents in Bangladesh over the next three years.

There was much more turbulence on our path ahead, ranging from cyber attacks, personal bankruptcy, personal failures, terror attacks, to just bad business decisions. At the end, it is not about the hurricanes themselves, but rather how we cope and learn from them is something that matters. We can plan, mitigate, reduce, and anticipate, yet the future is not written by us alone.

I have learned more about myself in the last four years than in my whole life put together. The last year, in particular, led me to a personal exponential journey by accepting my failures, coping with the disappointment, and facing the challenges without involving my ego. Only then was I able to see clearly and recognize how my own involvement had directly or indirectly shaped the company—was it the rather optimistic and naive timeline we had set to close a funding round, the belated and non-transparent communication with my team, or the lack of cultural understanding among my Bangladeshi former team members.

Being able to observe one's own past actions objectively holds more wisdom than any other recommendation. One may have the knowledge to build a toolkit, yet the ability to look at one's past failures, disappointments, and challenges as a gentle invitation to grow and prosper lies within oneself. I hold no grudge anymore against my former team, recognizing that their actions and beliefs were shaped by their prior experiences in my company. I do not blame myself for such an escalation but would rather shed more light at the darkness that I would have otherwise filled with negative emotions. This attitude has also set me free to understand that my actions in the past were driven by my ambition to build an organization with free minds, flat hierarchy, and open spirit. However, this enthusiasm was coupled with the lack of experience and skill set, which created a discrepancy between the goal and the reality. The flutter of a butterfly, as beautiful as it is, can create a hurricane. I caution you against taking impulsive actions to solve problems or to fix the issues: Stop for a minute, look around you to see clearly, and only then go ahead. Often, I did not have the foresight, patience, and mindfulness, which led me to an action that did not serve me or the company.

Starting a company and being aware of my actions taught me who I am and who I am not. I had seen myself as a strong leader, building an impactful company to help those in need. Keeping my ego aside, I now understand the discrepancy between who I desired to be and what my actual passion and skills are. Taking a personality test such as that offered by 16personalities.com supported this process and can be truly recommended. In fact, all new senior employees are now invited to share their personality types with the company, after which we have an open discussion about the results. This creates a transparent culture, where we know each other's strengths and weaknesses, which is crucial in the case of failures and disappointments.

I have not reached the top of my Mount Everest yet and I shall let go of the thought of not having reached the milestone and will focus on keep moving ahead. Then, once climbed, I will see a higher mountain that captures my attention and spurs me on—a restless loop that pulls me out of the present moment. We are enjoying a symphony, not by rushing to the final note, but rather through the unfolding of the music itself. With such sight, I can clearly see ahead and be anchored in the face of hardship and the many more hurricanes to come.

Economic and Policy Group: Perspectives on Building a Global Startup

One of our earliest global partners has been EPG in the UK, led by Pratik Dattani. I have signed a MoU with them to immerse EDUGILD's global companies in the UK and India. Pratik is very candid about his views on the entire global scale-up of Indian companies and has contributed his thoughts. Before that, let's discuss a little bit about EPG on the support they offer to companies.

- *Economic analysis:* What impact is regulation having on you? How can you advise policymakers to consider your points of view? EPG offer deep policy analysis to fit a company's requirements.
- *Market entry assistance:* Before entering a market, it is important to understand its business and cultural environment. Time, resources, and opportunities can be conserved with EPG's services.
- *Strategic communications:* How do you best communicate your organization's key messages to your stakeholders? Engaging customers or policymakers in the best possible manner is EPG's area of expertise.

Lessons for India's Innovation Ecosystem and the Startup Journey Abroad

London's startup ecosystem brings together talent, capital, innovation, and an openness to do business that few other cities in the world can match. However, it was not always known for its startups. After the financial downturn in 2008, Britain's politicians actively nurtured and established creative industries and tech hubs, starting with the formation of Tech City in London to introducing generous tax incentives for both entrepreneurs and investors. It represented a reinvention of sorts for the city, which had otherwise been overly dependent on financial services.

There is plenty that startup hubs in India can learn from such global success stories. Each of the most startup-friendly cities in the world have developed and nurtured their own unique model for supporting innovation. The European Digital City Index 2016 ranks Stockholm second after London in Europe for supporting entrepreneurs in the digital space thanks to the high penetration of fiber broadband, well-placed social welfare and safety standards allowing entrepreneurs to take risks, and easily identifiable role models such as Skype and Spotify.

What Silicon Valley is today did not develop spontaneously, but grew out of Stanford University leadership, availability of VC, university-led research, and support from the US Department of Defense Finance. In Tel Aviv, Israel, government schemes such as Yozma actively helped drive more entrepreneurial attitudes. It was a sovereign investment fund offering private investors insurance, covering 80 percent of the downside risk of investing.

Each city's development has one common thread: a structured approach, with the government at the heart of the transformation. This could take the form of accommodative policy, such as, the generous R&D tax credits, or institutional support through entrepreneurs' networks and other infrastructure. India could learn from some of these experiences in multiple ways.

Such policy or institutional changes are relatively straightforward to bring about over a 5- to 10-year period. They need a buy-in from a wide range of stakeholders and a zeal to implement across all levels of the government. Much of this is quiet work around building focus groups, nurturing networks, signposting opportunities for entrepreneurs, and anticipating what they may need to succeed. Positive PR is helpful, but the focus should be on the process of improvement rather just aiming for an announcement.

Then there is the cultural aspect: Is "tech startup entrepreneur" a recognized career choice for a young man or woman of marriageable age? We have a cultural intolerance to business failure and to giving someone who has failed once a second chance. Parents prefer their children to have steady jobs with low risk. The best innovation ecosystems in the world help de-risk failure, but this is more difficult in India, where a social safety net does not exist.

A more entrepreneurial outlook can, however, be nurtured through education. It is no coincidence that the world's innovation hubs have places of learning at their very center. India's education system needs to be more agile. More modern syllabi combined with entrepreneurship development classes and a much more robust tech transfer capability can go a long way.

Indian startups often also do not focus on the quality of product and prefer to launch even a half-baked product on schedule. In Silicon Valley, on the other hand, there is unrelenting focus on making the product appealing and the customer journey seamless. In India, coding takes priority over usability. It means not only that finding customers in India is more difficult, but also that Western markets—which will have many products with similar functionality, higher prices, but a better "feel"—are shut to such companies.

The government has the opportunity to act as a market maker in India for nurturing startups, but through a relentless focus on process, not publicity. For example, by providing startups preferential access to government projects, identifying urban development challenges where municipalities can source innovative startup ideas, and committing to clearing invoices within a reasonable timeframe.

Finally, Indian startups often lack global exposure. The Israeli, British, and US governments take startups on business delegations, provide exhibition opportunities at expos globally, and create international speaking opportunities, which, in India, are exclusively reserved for promoters and heads of big business houses. While this is done in some sectors, the Indian business chambers traditionally eschew this approach. This last area is one where EPG works the most. Building a global startup is of course possible without having an ecosystem in place, but the task is made much harder.

Many Indian startups coming to the UK are IT support service companies that want to find a freelance business developer to sell their product to on commission-only basis. It is difficult for such companies to succeed because they have not thought through why they want to be in the UK. A common response I hear is "we have some clients in the US, so we thought we should start in the UK."

At the same time, there are some exceptional Indian startups coming particularly to London to start their global journey. London offers the ecosystem benefits that parts of India may not; some of these benefits are ease of doing business, being able to incorporate a company in minutes, generous R&D tax breaks, access to finance and markets, and the opportunity to expand into a global business using London as a base, sometimes with formal UK government support.

The most interesting companies to work with are those with a long-term vision. They understand the difference between a trusted advisor and an in-country reseller, and therefore value strategic advice. EPG works with the founders to help them understand the market, including who their competitors are, the right avenues to enter the market, and how to build a sustainable long-term presence. There may be government grants or other incentives from regional development agencies available to help manage the inevitable costs associated with UK market entry. The basics of setting up a business, of accounting and legal support, finding an office, and ensuring that the right work visa is applied for are all part of the role of a trusted advisor.

London is a competitive place for international startups, all jostling for attention. The presence of a vibrant ecosystem means that although there are many smart entrepreneurs with a good product and an identified market, some of them may fail because the sales cycles are too long for them to afford being sustainable, or they lack the necessary working capital, or they are not able to stand apart from the crowd.

Building a brand through events, speaking opportunities, being featured in industry reports, meetings with senior decision-makers, and being seen at the right places can often be just as important. These avenues for growth do not represent a linear path to sales, such as, running a Facebook or Google AdWords marketing campaign, which a product company can do without leaving the shores of India. However, they do increase a startup's exposure to "black swans," which are extremely rare but high-impact events, often inappropriately rationalized *ex-post* with the benefit of hindsight. They also help the management team understand the local market context beyond just what a research report might say. This is in part the cultural challenge I discussed before, but also a small-to-medium enterprise phenomenon that equally applies to British small-to-medium enterprises looking to enter the Indian market. The role of a trusted advisor is not one that can be boxed into accountancy support, business development strategy, or PR. It means understanding the founder's vision, proactively identifying gaps in their knowledge, and helping build a business that can scale up internationally. Understanding the basic building blocks of new markets is in many ways straightforward, but it takes time, application, and sheer will.

KnowHassles: A Thought-provoking Global Scale-up Experience

My engagement with KnowHassles has been another thought-provoking global scale-up experience. KnowHassles was initiated in the year 2015 to help international students get all post-landing services under one roof. The company, incorporated in Toronto, Canada, started its operations with a basic webpage and a master business license, headed by Harshad and Harshad, the two founders of the company with the same first names.

The venture involved Indian students, their visa consultants, and post-landing service providers in Toronto. To start with, KnowHassles looked for partnership opportunities in India as well as in Canada. In the year 2016, they partnered with Edwise International, a well-known foreign education consultancy in India, which has branches in 18 different cities in India and sends students worldwide for higher studies. KnowHassles' offering was added benefit to Edwise's on-going services, and hence both parties mutually agreed to operate on a revenue-sharing model.

Being new to the market, KnowHassles took cautious steps and did not push themselves too much to get tied up with more such consultants. Now the focus shifted to Canadian service providers. The services varied from accommodation to day-to-day tiffin facilities, and hence KnowHassles looked for two to three vendors of each service to work on a revenue-sharing model again. Their partners' list consisted of well-known realtors, Uber drivers, and top telecom and Internet providers in Toronto.

In the year 2017, KnowHassles served around 70 students in three intakes. They charged minimal fees to students to avail the services they needed and also covered third-party commission from the local Torontonian vendors. However, the major challenge was currency exchange. Money was being collected in Indian rupees as well as in Canadian dollars. Students could not transfer the rent amounts quickly, being expatriates. Hence, to avoid delays, KnowHassles opened an NRI account in India that could handle multiple currencies. Their website also had third-party wallet integration (such as PayPal). KnowHassles took care of fresh international students' government IDs and bank-opening processes by taking students to the government offices and preparing their documents in Canadian format.

KnowHassles is continuously improving its offering and guidance to help Indian students settle down quickly in Toronto. The guidance provided by them is very important for fresh students and prepares them to represent themselves and India in a proper manner at the global stage.

SkillSoniq: Matching Skilled Consultants with Financial Institutions

Moving forward, I am very tempted to include my experience with another portfolio company, SkillSoniq, founded by Abhinav Verma and based in New York. Abhinav has been leveraging his roots in India for product development, and his presence in the USA for creating a market there. Upon my insistence, he agreed to share the company's story as an evidence of risk, initiative, and perseverance. Read through, as Abhinav stated.

I founded SkillSoniq in New York, USA, in 2017 to match pre-screened contingent workers with financial institutions using intelligent algorithms and smart curation techniques. With our back-end operations set up in India, and the sales and marketing activities in the USA, I aspire to build a truly global venture. My journey has not been easy so far, but I am determined to build a successful venture to solve a problem that has been ongoing for decades. I currently live with my wife in New York.

After completing high school from India, I moved to the USA to pursue higher studies. I graduated at the top of my class with an undergraduate business degree from the prestigious Ross School of Business at the University of Michigan. Before starting SkillSoniq, I gained 10+ years of experience across India and the USA as an investment banker, strategy and operations consultant, and an entrepreneur in the education and training space. Having worked in both the eastern and western hemispheres, I understand the opportunities and challenges that exist in today's global marketplace.

SkillSoniq is a culmination of the problems I faced in securing a contract role with banks in the USA. After multiple attempts and several months of work, I could not secure a contract role with a bank, despite having significant experience and skills. That is when I realized that this was not because of my experience or lack of it, but because of a flawed "staffing-agency-led" recruitment process, which failed to understand and highlight my credentials to the clients.

Over 30 percent of the American labor force consists of contingent workers, and almost all of them are hired through traditional staffing agencies. This practice dates back to the Second World War, when the concept of staffing agencies was born to put women to work in a formal capacity. Agencies were created to hire women on their payroll, and "lease" them out to companies at a hefty margin. Over time, the roles covered expanded to include higher skilled jobs, and more agencies cropped up to staff both men and women in the job market. Over the last 75 years, while the population of contingent workers has grown in the USA, the process of staffing them has not kept up with the changing times, resulting in inefficiencies in the contingent worker recruitment process.

Through SkillSoniq, my vision is to build a recruitment app that delivers the most skilled contingent workers to financial institutions in the shortest time using machine learning and AI techniques, akin to how Uber delivers cars to passengers. By doing this, I hope to help contingent workers get their next project quickly, and my clients execute million-dollar projects through the workers I provide. I am working to solve three key pain points in this space:

1. Over 50 percent of contingent worker resumes are poorly worded and structured, leading to delay in recruitment.
2. Over 50 percent of contingent workers are rejected in the first round by end clients due to poor screening of skills upfront by staffing agencies.
3. It takes contingent workers over three months to find their next project, as they depend on mediocre "human" recruiters (hired by staffing agencies of course!) to find them a project.

Through SkillSoniq, I am building a recruitment market-place that screens contingent workers, curates their skills and experiences in an easy-to-understand format, and automatically connects them with relevant projects posted by clients. My goal is to make it easier for clients to make a hiring decision and cut down their hiring time from months to days, at the same time providing a way for contingent workers to manage their project life cycle from their first project to their next from a central application. We operate in the financial services space, since financial institutions are one of the largest employers of temporary labor in the USA, and since I have a rich background in financial services.

As an immigrant in the USA, starting and building a company has not been easy for me. In addition to the challenges faced by any entrepreneur (irrespective of location), operating in the USA as a foreigner comes with its own set of difficulties. So much so that I have often contemplated moving back to India, and have had countless discussions with close friends and family on the pros and cons of shifting base. Over time, I have realized though that having a base in the USA has actually been more advantageous for SkillSoniq, and will help me in building a global venture in the future.

First off, navigating through visa legalities and processes in the "Donald Trump era" has been hard. I have had to consult several lawyers, friends, and colleagues to understand the existing visa landscape, and on setting up my company the right way as an immigrant. While the visa system in the USA is not set up to promote immigrant entrepreneurs, there are thousands of Indians in the USA who have found loopholes around the law and are now running fledgling companies. Despite this, only about 1 percent of the immigrant Indians I know here run their own companies, while the remaining 99 percent are content with a job. Being part of the 1 percent in my close network of friends has definitely not been easy, and it makes me feel that I am working against the odds when I wake up every morning.

Perhaps as important, if not more, as setting up a company the right way was to build an initial tech team for SkillSoniq. This was especially important for me as I come from a non-technical background and SkillSoniq is a tech-heavy platform. Over the last 12 months, I have worked with five potential tech co-founders in India and the USA. The candidates I worked with in the USA demanded a salary to work with me, while the candidates in India did not have a US work permit, but wanted a way to work in the USA. While I invested a lot of time and energy in all five potential co-founders, none of them worked out for me. At times like this, I wished I had a startup in India, where I could find tech friends to work with me.

After a lot of thought, I decided to outsource tech development for two major reasons:

1. This would allow me to quickly test my concept and eventually hire an in-house tech team.
2. This would allow me to earn in dollars while cutting my R&D and tech costs (down to 20% of what it is in the USA) in the future.

After spending several months working with web development agencies in Manila, India, and Ukraine, I decided to home in on an agency in India. One of the challenges of working with a team in India is the time difference of 10.5 hours. While I work on the sales and marketing activities in the day, I am on calls with my tech team at night and early in the morning. Although this schedule can get exhausting, having back-end tech operations in India allows me to have close ties at home and work with really smart engineers at one-fifth the cost.

Over time, I realized that the advantages of setting up SkillSoniq in the USA are manifold. Staying in the USA has also allowed me to stay in close connect with financial institutions and understand trends in the contingent worker hiring process, especially because Western countries such as the USA and the UK are leaders in this space. Operating out of the USA has also allowed me to partner with top engineering and business schools as well as with staffing agencies to build my database of skilled contingent workers. With the US companies such as Uber and Airbnb having pioneered the concept of democratization of labor, staying in the USA has allowed me to network with the right stakeholders and really understand business models that have been successful in the west.

Today, my core team consists of a project manager, a full-stack developer, a UI/UX designer in India, and a lead recruiter in the USA. We have successfully partnered with the University of Phoenix and the Tuck School of Business at Dartmouth University to place their over 100,000 alumni in contract roles. We have also partnered with five staffing agencies to place their bench of consultants in contract roles in the USA. We are currently working to build our initial cohort of paid customers before we look to scale up. In the next few years, I hope to build a global company by first proving myself to the USA, and then expanding my operations and customer base to other parts of the world.

Global EdTech Impact: The Israeli Perspective

[By Dr Jacob (Yaki) Dayan, Founder and CEO, EdTech Israel]

Edtech is globally recognized as an immense opportunity. The synergy between talents, technologies, and social goals is fueling this multibillion industry. Edtech has become a global phenomenon with national manifestations. The global edtech ecosystem encompasses numerous national ecosystems—each country or nation has a different ecosystem, different approach, and different way to interact with similar ecosystems around the world.

The state of Israel has a worldwide reputation for innovation, creativity, and the startup mentality. Mobileye, Waze, Kaltura, Wix, and Fiverr are just a few examples of companies that started in Israel and are going global. The startup mentality, vibrant VC community, and abundance of acceleration and incubation programs are a blessing for every Israeli edtech entrepreneur.

Education is not an easy market to be in. A lot has been discussed about the long lead times for business and returns, the complex business models, and the fragmentation in this segment. Unlike big markets such as the USA, India, or even the UK, the local market in Israel is non-existent. With only about 2 million students, and 80 percent of the content in Hebrew, the Israeli education market is not a business opportunity for startups, and often cannot be even a good beta site before international expansion. Moreover, when edtech startups approach VCs in Israel, they compete against startups from IoT, smart transportation, cyber, and so many other sectors that are way more attractive for the VC community. Hence, the edtech startup ecosystem in Israel is quite challenging.

EdTech Israel was established in September 2014 with the vision of disrupting and reshaping the local ecosystem, and forming a bridge to connect it to the global edtech ecosystem. By analyzing the uniqueness of the local ecosystem and forecasting global trends and opportunities, the methods of operation they engage in are different from other national ecosystem builders.

In Israel, there are so many acceleration programs to choose from. Many of them are free, take no equity, and offer excellent mentors and rich training programs. An Israeli edtech startup in pre-seed stage can choose between the prestigious 8200 accelerator in Tel Aviv or the international MassChallenge program in Jerusalem. Startups in Stage A or beyond can opt for the IBM accelerator in Haifa or the Microsoft accelerator in Tel Aviv. What EDUGILD offers in addition is strategic advice and mentorship that is edtech-focused, and complement the offering of general-purpose accelerators.

What Israeli edtech startups need the most are two things: funding and international expansion. This is what EdTech Israel is focusing on. As a nationwide, unbiased entity, EdTech Israel is connected to over 30 international venture capitalists that are interested in innovative edtech solutions. For Israeli edtech startups, the likelihood of receiving a seed or an investment from international venture capitalists is much higher than that from a local venture capitalist.

The focus on international expansion is another key factor that sets Israeli edtech startups apart from their peers in other countries. From the word "go", they face issues such as multi-language support, supporting clients in multiple time zones, and adopting business models that fit international markets. This makes them more likely to form international partnerships, make an impact in developing countries, and form joint ventures or distribution channels in several countries.

The Israeli EdTech Summit (IES) is a platform that is addressing this need for international expansion. Edtech summits around the globe afford international relationships, knowledge sharing, and impact. To achieve this, in 2016, EdTech Israel established the Israeli EdTech Summit (IES) with two significant partners: one is EastWind Advisors, a strong investment banking firm from New York, USA, and the other is the Tel Aviv University (TAU), a strong reputable academic partner. IES has quickly become a huge success and a national asset for the local edtech ecosystem. IES2017, held in Tel Aviv in June 2017, attracted over 90 international speakers and delegates from 15 nations. They arrived at Tel Aviv for two days to meet over 50 edtech startups, joining 180 Israeli entrepreneurs and 460 attendees from educational institutes, the VC community, social impact leaders, and industry experts. IES2018 is planned for June 6–7, 2018, in Tel Aviv.

The international collaboration extends to edtech business delegations as well. Starting with the first edtech delegation to Brazil in 2015, EdTech Israel organized delegations to Asia (Thailand, Vietnam), China, and the UK. For international delegations and companies seeking business with the Israeli edtech companies, they facilitate meeting startups, mature companies, innovation hubs, and educational institutes. So far, they have hosted delegates and businesses from China, India, Argentina, France, the UK, the USA, Brazil, Germany, etc. As stated by Dr Yaki Dayan, Founder, EdTech Israel, "the Israeli edtech ecosystem is developing now, and growing rapidly. The global edtech ecosystem is developing as well, and we are grateful for the opportunity to contribute our share in reshaping education around the world."

It all comes down to ensuring that startups have their vision set to being viable beyond barriers. This is a thought shift and makes startups put the cogs in place to go beyond borders. With the telecom and Internet landscape, being globally present is easy but being a global company in culture, revenue, and reach is an enormous challenge. The global mindset would also need startups to identify the advantages and liabilities of starting an international company and to know how to manage it locally and coordinate with various time zones along with building partnerships and personal networks. Each company must choose its global battlefront very carefully in order to acquire the methods and tools to enable ventures in more parts of the world.

About the Author

Rishi Kapal, a Stanford LEADer, is currently the Global Strategist and CEO of EDUGILD Global Edtech Accelerator. His academic and entrepreneurial journey started in 2013, initially as a teacher of Sales, IMC and Entrepreneurship at leading management colleges. Presently, Rishi holds a portfolio of more than 20 edtech companies, invested in sweat equity as a business strategist and sales facilitator. Within 24 months of his association, couple of Rishi's portfolio startups have reached a monthly revenue rate of 5–8 lakhs and have raised funds close to ₹10 crore in all.

From 1993 to 2013, over two decades, Rishi helmed strategic and operational roles in Sony, Qualcomm, Ericsson, BP/Castrol, Avaya, and HCL. Having received several awards and accolades for his professionalism and speed of execution, his last corporate assignment was as the VP and Interim MD of Sony Mobile Communications, owning a business deliverable of over USD200M.

As a senior coach with Right Management, Rishi conducts career transitions, experiences and performance management engagement sessions. His beneficiaries include super-senior and middle-management leadership teams of multinationals and students of educational institutes.

Rishi has been an invited speaker at the United Nations HQ in New York and has travelled and learned extensively from his global journeys. He speaks at various international forums and is also a published author. He has co-authored research papers with laureates of Oxford University and IIT Kharagpur. Academically,

Rishi has dabbled in many fields. He is an Electronics Engineer and a Law Graduate. He also holds a master's degree in marketing management from Pune University and is a post-graduate in management from IMI and on-boarded LEAD Certificate Program (one year) from Stanford University's Graduate School of Business.

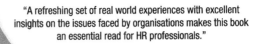

CPSIA information can be obtained
at www.ICGtesting.com
Printed in the USA
LVHW111439171218
600747LV00001B/221/P